PROJECT:
ORGANIZATION

PROJECT:
ORGANIZATION

Quick and Easy Ways to Organize Your Life

MARIE RICKS

SHADOW
MOUNTAIN

Front cover images:
Mobile phone, notebooks and leather bag on chair: © ML Harris/ Iconica/Getty Images
Houseplant on table: © Michael Bader/ Westend61/Getty Images
Kitchen utensils: © MIXA/Getty Images

Back cover images:
Laundry and detergent: © Joanna Zopoth-Lipiejko/Shutterstock
Kitchen: © Natalia V Guseva/Shutterstock
Tools: © Elnur/Shutterstock

Organize Your Home:
File folders: © Alex Hinds/Shutterstock
Kitchen sink: © Elena Elisseeva/Shutterstock
Clothes on hangers: © Hannamariah/Shutterstock

Organize Your Family:
Boy doing homework: © Nicholas Sutcliffe/Shutterstock
Family: © digitalskillet/Shutterstock
Girl sitting on soccer ball: © Sean Bolt/Shutterstock

Organize Your Time:
Alarm clock: © Paul Turner/Shutterstock
Calendar: © iofoto/Shutterstock
Purse with planner and pen: © matka_Wariatka/Shutterstock

Organize Your Other Important Occasions:
Airplane: © Robert Hackett/Shutterstock
Balloons and candles: © Glen Jones/Shutterstock
Boxes: © Brian McEntire/Shutterstock

Graphic illustration on page xii © 2007 Thomas Earl Ricks

Visit us at ShadowMountain.com

Library of Congress Cataloging-in-Publication Data
Ricks, Marie.
   Project organization : quick and easy ways to organize your life / Marie Ricks.
      p.   cm.
   ISBN 978-1-59038-796-2 (pbk.)
   1. Home economics.   2. Housekeeping.   I. Title.
TX147.R48 2007
640—dc22   2007018386

Printed in the United States of America
Publishers Printing, Salt Lake City, Utah

10   9   8   7   6   5   4   3   2   1

To my husband, Jim,

who is the inspiration of my life and soul;

my sons—Tom, David, Brian, Tyler, and Evan—

who have filled my life with joy;

and Jenn, my new daughter-in-law,

who brings hope for the future

Contents

Organize Your Home

KITCHEN

CONTENTS

LAUNDRY

GARAGE

HOME OFFICE

Organize Your Family

CHILDREN

Organize Your Time

SEASONS AND HOLIDAYS

Organize Your Other Important Occasions

Acknowledgments

Saying thank you is never easy because so many people do so much behind the scenes and without fanfare, but specifically I would like to render gratitude to my husband, children, and extended family for their consistent and unending support during the writing of this book.

There are many others who have helped, too, including each and every person I have met who has shared with me their own life's struggle and triumphs to find a more orderly life. They will remain anonymous, but they are the reason for this book finding its way to fruition.

Thanks to Thomas E. Ricks for sharing his graphic art skills on the next page.

I also appreciate the team at Shadow Mountain for their contributions, including Jana Erickson for heading the project, Lisa Mangum for editing the concepts which I wished to share, Sheryl Dickert Smith for a beautiful cover and design, Tonya Facemyer for typesetting, and Mary Ann Jones for her public relations expertise.

To you all, I say a hearty thanks!

Introduction

I love to help people get organized. Over and over again, whether I'm teaching classes, speaking to groups, or coaching one-on-one, I have seen people's lives dramatically change for the better as they become more organized. Overwhelmed housewives find they can function at a higher level in keeping their homes at a reasonable level of cleanliness, even as they pursue other interests. Working women find great capacity to face the long weeks and the wearying weekends. Teenagers gain organizational skills that will help them as their responsibilities increase and will empower them to achieve greater victories in life. Men do better professionally and have a happier home life.

While all of us are in a unique situation and in a singular season of life, all of us have challenges with disorder. It is just part of living. There is much we can do to overcome chaos in our lives, however, and this book is a great beginning. It addresses common, everyday problems we all face as we maintain a home, deal with family members, hold down a job, and handle the stresses in life.

Life can be hard. But we can learn to make it easier. The principles of organization are available to everyone. Come with me to a place of wisdom, action, and change. In the process you will find a better, more orderly life!

Understanding Organization

Before we tackle getting more organized, we need to lay a good foundation for success.

There are two main kinds of organization. Organization of *items* includes such tasks as setting up the laundry room, sorting through your bedroom closet, cleaning out the pantry, or fixing up your garage workshop. This is the preliminary stage of organization, the kind we do when things have gone from bad to worse and we are finally ready to *act*. This type of organization is a vital beginning to creating a more orderly life.

Organization of *routines* includes such processes as washing and drying the laundry, filing paperwork, or cleaning the kitchen after dinner. These are more mundane tasks, but are highly essential organizational routines that keep our lives happy and productive.

Getting Organized, Staying Organized

There are also two main steps to organization: First, we want to *get* organized, and second, we want to *stay* organized. These are two very different—but important—steps of organization.

GETTING ORGANIZED → STAYING ORGANIZED

Getting organized usually involves the organization of items: cleaning out a junky kitchen drawer so it becomes more usable, working through a huge stack of paperwork and getting it all filed, or sorting through your children's crowded clothes closet and packing away those items that are too small, too big, or simply unusable.

All of these "getting organized" projects then become part of your daily routine as "staying organized" projects: sorting through the items in the kitchen drawer to keep it workable, filing papers on a frequent basis to keep your home office neat, or teaching your children to manage their clothes closet as they grow out of their current wardrobe and into a new one.

Staying organized also involves the organization of routines: getting the wash done, dried, folded, and put away; finishing the dinner dishes at night; or straightening the bathroom after a family member has showered.

Tools, Systems, and Routines

As we look at any organizational project, there are three elements of organization that must be a part of our plan in order to move to a place of greater order: tools, systems, and routines.

TOOLS → SYSTEMS → ROUTINES

TOOLS

You have a pile of clothes bound for the thrift store, but how will you get them there without a sturdy box or an oversized garbage bag to transport them? You sit down to organize your paperwork, but how will you keep track of all the papers without file folders, a marking pen, and a place for filing? You have messy kitchen drawers, but how will you organize them without dividers?

Having the right tools at hand is the essential first step in organizing both items and routines. Boxes, folders, containers, dividers—whatever tools you need to prepare for this first step must be purchased or found. As you gather the tools that work best for you and your projects, you can begin to divide, confine, and conquer.

SYSTEMS

Deciding upon a system that will work for you is essential to keeping your initial organization just the way you want it. Anything you diligently organize will disorganize itself unless you have a system in place to maintain that organization—to "stay organized." Now that you have the paperwork under control, what system will you use to keep up with the paperwork? Will you train your family to put the latest homework papers in an "in" box so they can be sorted on a daily basis? Will you inform your spouse that the mail can now be found in a stackable tray by the door? What will be your method for handling the mail each day? Asking these kinds of questions and discovering their answers are important steps in implementing systems that will help you stay organized.

ROUTINES

Routines are absolutely essential to maintaining the organization you have so diligently started. You might have good tools, you might have set up a system that works for you, but if you don't include organizing and maintaining into your routines, things will fall apart on their own. You have to set aside regular times in your schedule to keep up on the organization you have put in place. Remember, it takes a lot of work to be organized, but it takes a lot more work to be disorganized. Why not choose the easier way?

Circles of Organization

This brings us to the circles of order and disorder. Visualize a circle with order (O) at the top and disorder (D) at the bottom. The "O" stands for organization. The "D" stands for disorganization.

ORDER (O)

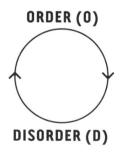

DISORDER (D)

In life, we work very hard to get organized and move to the top of the circle, but then we fix a meal and the kitchen gets dirty, the dishes are in the sink, and the table is cluttered. Every time we change our clothes, take a shower, or get ready for bed, we move from the top of the organization circle down and around to disorganization at the bottom of the circle. It takes a great effort to keep moving around the circle back up to order again, but if we are to stay organized, move we must.

FINISHING WHAT WE START

When we finish the meal by doing the dishes, wiping down the counter tops, and sweeping up the crumbs under the table, or when we gather the dirty clothes, do the laundry, and put the clothes away, we move back up to the top of the organization circle before we begin to move around the circle again.

As I observed women who seemed to be more organized, I discovered they move around their organization circles from order to disorder back to order again without getting stuck at the bottom of the circle. They make a mess as they fix lunch, but then they stay until their kitchen is ordered again. After they start the wash, they keep at it until the laundry is put away. They get out a project but don't abandon it when other priorities call; they clean it up and put it away first.

In other words, we may be juggling multiple circles of organization, but we shouldn't stay at the bottom of any one circle and let inertia trap us there in a place of disorder. We need to learn to *finish*. If we don't leave the dishes undone after breakfast, or the clean clothes unfolded on the couch, or an ongoing creative project on the table when we leave to pick up the kids from school, we will always be traveling toward the top of our organization circle.

This simple habit of finishing what we start will enable us to have more order in our lives. It allows us the freedom to have some messes out, but not have the whole house be a mess.

Because we are so very busy, many of us may be moving around a lot of organization circles at the same time. We get breakfast started, then we wake up the baby, start a batch of wash, say good-bye as our spouse leaves for work, and finally we send the kids off to school. It is important as we do our routines that we keep moving around the organization circles back to order: wipe off the table after breakfast while the kids are getting their coats on for school, move the laundry to the dryer while our spouse is finding his or her laptop for work, make our bed while the baby is playing quietly, and pick up the stray items from the hallway as we walk down it.

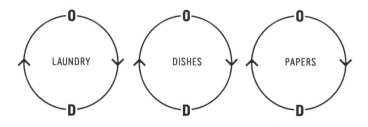

Remember, as we *finish* our projects, we continue to move around our organization circles until we end up at the top of the circle again.

PRIORITIES

So many of us have grand ideas we want to act upon, but we often neglect to set our households in order first so that we are organized enough to successfully focus on our other projects and still maintain order in our lives. In other words, we don't first finish our foundational organization circles before we focus on other ones. We don't get the wash started, the breakfast dishes done, or the baby dressed before we decide to begin baking bread, call our friend to go shopping in the afternoon, or get out our scrapbooking project.

It is indispensable for us to have a regular routine for getting our day started—taking a shower and getting dressed, getting the kids up and fed—before we begin other priorities. As you well know, often if you don't start the day out right, it's harder to handle the pressures of the day. So

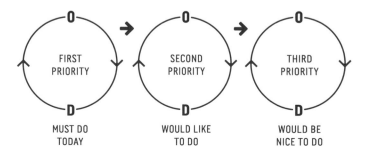

take a moment and identify the three most important organizational routines that need to be a part of *your* morning—every morning.

As you master these three organizational routines, you will find it easier to add more circles—more routines—to your day. Remember, it is important not to start more circles than you are able to finish in one day. With practice, you will develop the ability to gauge how much time you think the pressures of the day will demand and balance that against the amount of time you have to start, work on, and bring to a finishing point a given project. In general, err on the side of too few circles. It is better to start less and finish more than to start too much and not finish anything.

Also, doing housework, dishes, laundry, paperwork, and any other household chores sooner rather than later will keep the circles of our organization smaller and tighter. It is always easier to wipe down the kitchen counter frequently than to have to scrub off hardened food. It is easier to do laundry every day than once a week in a washing marathon. It is nicer to handle the mail every day instead of worrying about unpaid bills and filing a stack of paperwork once a month.

As you select your own organization circles, consider keeping your routines frequent, with short, small periods of intense focus instead of long, less frequent sessions of tedious organization.

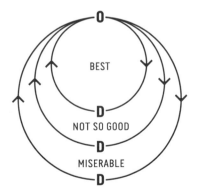

Conclusion

Having shared some thoughts about the theory behind personal, household, and family organization, it's time to begin. The rest of this book focuses on specific organizational projects. You'll identify the necessary tools to acquire, the systems to consider, and the routines to establish that will bring your life closer to the order you desire. You'll also learn practical ways to make the special events in your life more remarkable, concepts to incorporate into your routines, and ideas to apply to your everyday life. Remember, the orderly way is the easier way. It might take a lot of work to get started, but once your organizational circles are spinning, it is so well worth the trouble. And, in the end, life will be easier. Good luck!

ORGANIZE YOUR HOME

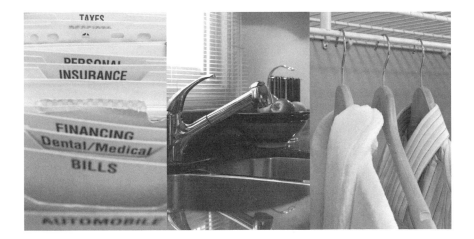

1

"Neating" Before Cleaning

There is a better way to organize your housework and clean your house. It is easy to explain, a bit harder to implement, and even harder to wonder why you didn't start doing this a long time ago. Are you ready? Let's go!

First, there are three basic kinds of cleaning: "neating" (which is usually done every day), cleaning (which is usually done between once a day and once a week), and scrubbing (which is done less often, usually monthly, semiannually, or annually).

Neating is *not* really *cleaning* at all, but it sure gives the illusion of cleanliness. Neating is making the house look clean by simply picking up, putting away, and otherwise straightening. The best way to accomplish the daily task of neating is to acquire a cobbler's apron with two large pockets. One pocket is for "keeps"—small items that have been misplaced and need to be put back in their "homes." The other pocket is for garbage—items that can later be deposited in a wastebasket. You can also use a small divided basket or bag instead. The idea is to be able to quickly divide the "keeps" from the "trash."

First thing every morning, after breakfast is finished and you have your spouse ready for work, your kids ready for school, and almost everyone out the door, put on that apron and go to work.

Begin with the kitchen. Clear the table and load the dishes into the dishwasher, close all the cupboard doors, wipe down the counters and sweep up the crumbs, and push in the chairs around the table.

Then move to the front door, as the entryway is the most important place to keep presentable, and make the living room and family room a top priority; then work through the house from there. Pick up the "keeps" and put them in one pocket; deposit trash in the other pocket. Large objects that are out of place will have to be carried separately to their rightful homes. For now, simply sort the large objects into piles based on which room they belong in and move them to their rightful rooms in a second pass through the house. Straighten pillows, open curtains, put away magazines, and collect empty soda cans; make each room look as nice as you can with this first neating pass.

When you get to the bedrooms, make the beds (if you haven't already taught your children to finish that chore before they go to school), pick up larger stray items and deposit them where they belong, open the curtains and blinds, and shut the closet doors.

In the bathroom, straighten the items on the counter, wipe out the sink with the swish of a damp cloth, flush the toilet and close the lid, straighten the towels on the rack, pick up any stray items, close the shower curtain, and straighten the rug. Again, the idea is to leave the room looking as neat as you can as quickly as you can.

In your own bedroom, do the same maintenance routine: make the bed, open the curtains or blinds, pick up and hang stray clothes, and straighten the items on the top of the dresser. No deep cleaning needs to be done just yet, just neating, straightening, and putting things back where they belong.

Now, walk around the house one more time to make sure your neating is done. Empty your apron pocket of trash into the wastebasket. Deposit the small items you have collected in an "organization jar" (usually an oversized container in a cupboard conveniently located in your kitchen), and then hang up your apron on its hook, ready for tomorrow's neating.

When your organization jar is full, you can have an organization party. Using muffin tins or small baskets to sort items, you can involve your children in separating and putting away the myriad of small treasures you've collected from your daily neating.

Remember, most spouses, children, or company do not readily see dirt and grime. They are more readily aware of the neatness of your home. And you will find that a neat home is nicer to live in and easier to clean, freeing up time for you to tackle the deep-cleaning jobs your home may require.

The most important *first* part of housework is the picking up part. So begin each day with a habit of "neating before cleaning." In a matter of minutes you'll find your housework is easier, the house looks nicer, and your mood is better, because if unexpected company drops in, you'll be able to welcome them into a nice, neat home.

2

Launching and Landing Pads

One of the best ways to organize your life at home or at work is to designate launching and landing pads. Identifying launching and landing pads for your home will require designating a place, implementing a method, and reserving a few minutes of time in your daily schedule to successfully "launch" or "land."

Life is constantly in motion, and to stay organized during the day we need temporary resting places for the items in our lives as we transition from one activity to another. For instance, suppose you purchase a valance for your kitchen window during the week, but you won't be able to unwrap it, hang a rod, and put it up until the weekend. Where will you keep the valance until Saturday? The space you designate is called the landing pad.

Before Saturday, though, you decide you don't like the valance after all and need to return it. Where will you keep it so you'll remember to take it with you the next time you run errands? This space is called the launching pad.

It is important to have specified launching and landing pads at home and at the workplace. The pads can be anywhere in your home, but the

14

space should be a flat surface in a contained area that is left empty except for "landed" items.

Your landing pad might be a basket near your back door, or a shelf in the laundry room or closet. It might even be in a kitchen cupboard with shelves labeled "Projects to Do," "Items to Address," and "Things to Worry About Later." Since we usually land the same items each and every time we return home—car keys, the daily mail, a purse or wallet—this will be a well-used place, so think carefully about the traffic patterns in your home and choose a convenient and accessible landing space.

Likewise, there needs to be a place for launching. This is a space where you can put items you need to take anytime you leave the house: when you run errands, when you go a meeting, or when you have another obligation. This designated launching pad is where we keep "Items to Return," "Books for the Library," and "Items to Take to Grandma's House."

Both launching and landing shelves are reserved for these specific purposes, allowing us a convenient repository for our belongings when we come home from running errands, as well as a safe haven for items that we want to take with us the next time we leave home.

Once we have chosen locations for our launching and landing pads, we must think about the methods we use for setting things aside and for gathering things up. It is essential to keep your landing pad as empty as possible by taking a few moments to put away, file, or throw away the items you've landed. Otherwise, the landing pad becomes a landing *closet* and eventually a landing *room*. So, as part of the launching and landing concept, we must not just purchase and put aside, we must address and complete. The valance can sit in the landing pad for a while, but it also needs to be hung up or returned.

It is also important to acquire and organize the tools for launching, especially for the repetitive routines in your life. For most people, it is helpful to have a sturdy, oversized bag or other container for each regularly repeated activity or project. For instance, there might be a preschool teaching bag filled with a manual, visual aids, crayons, and extra paper; another bag with toys and books to read to children while waiting at the doctor's office or for piano lessons to finish; even a special bag for yourself with a book and a crocheting project to take with you while you are wait-ing to get your hair done.

Finally, successful home managers plan for and allow time for launch-ing and landing. Launching is the hardest to do because we are usually so stressed and in such a hurry to leave that we often don't have the time to think through our day thoroughly. That means launching from our shelf to our vehicle is best done early: tonight for tomorrow morning's needs, in the morning for an afternoon appointment, today for tonight's needs. In addition, try to allow a few extra minutes before leaving to mentally review your launching needs because you will usually think of some last-minute "to do's."

Also, allow time to "land" after you come home from an activity, a project, or another commitment. It takes just a few minutes to clean out the vehicle, put the items where they belong, and finish "coming home." Removing your library books from the car, putting them away in their rightful places, and hanging up your coat are all habits of "landing" in the right way.

When we set aside the space and time for launching and landing, we will find that "L&L" can be one of the most successful habits of a more orderly life.

3

Pick It Up—Don't Pass It By

I am often asked how to cope with family members who quickly disorganize any organization that has been done. Children who don't pick up their toys or clothes, teenagers who seem to cause messes just by whisking through a room, and spouses who might put things away but maybe not in a timely manner are all part of the problem. It can drive a home manager crazy!

I believe everyone who lives in the house should help keep the house in order. Remember, you are the home manager, not the maid!

As the home manager, begin by having a training session with the whole family where you can introduce the new standard: Pick it up—don't pass it by. Then practice by having the children leave the room one at a time to find something that is out of place somewhere in the house. Ask them to return with the item and indicate to you where it is to go. When they have successfully put it away and returned, reward them with a special treat. Have each child, from oldest to youngest, practice this activity at least once.

Announce that there will be a reward system set up for family members who help pick up and put things away *in the right place* on a daily basis. The reward system can be as simple as placing Popsicle sticks (or buttons or paper clips) from a general family jar in the children's individual jars when they have reported to you something that they put away voluntarily.

Then, after dinner each night for a week, Mom or Dad exchanges the Popsicle sticks in each family member's jar for a sweet treat (M&Ms, for example) as dessert. The empty individual jars are put back on a shelf, ready to be filled again the next day.

If a child or teenager is asked to pick something up and doesn't do it willingly, simply take a stick out of his or her jar and put it back in the family jar.

Try this for a week and you'll notice immediate success. As the family embraces the "pick it up—don't pass it by" principle, change the reward from a sweet treat or candy for each item to something where they must do more for less: for example, ten Popsicle sticks in their personal jar can be exchanged for one small candy bar, or twenty sticks are worth some special one-on-one time with Mom. Be creative with the rewards, but keep it up until everyone is picking up after themselves all the time out of habit.

Instilling this principle in your family is one of the best things you can do to have a more organized and orderly home.

4

If You Care, Keep a Spare

One way for any home manager to save lots of time is to have an extra of everything you use regularly stored somewhere in your house. A good organizational goal is to always have a spare on hand—always! There is an easy two-part method you can implement immediately that will keep you content, knowing that the extra item is just downstairs or in the cupboard or in the garage, as well as knowing when it is time to get another one.

The first step in the process is to designate a "Spares Box" in your home. Any box, bucket, or bin will work—but remember to keep it clearly labeled and easily accessible. Then, as your budget allows, simply buy two of something instead of only one and store the second item in the "Spares Box." When your watch battery needs to be replaced, purchase a second one, date and label it, and store it in the box. When your computer printer cartridge runs dry, buy one to use and one to put away. When the kitchen timer breaks, buy two.

Because you are doubling up on several of your shopping items, you may find an increased amount of free time in your schedule because your replacements are conveniently located in a "Spares Box" in the kitchen, garage, or bedroom closet instead of requiring a special trip to the store.

No more extra errands to the store to buy just one item. Instead, you can simply go back to work printing a letter, setting your watch to the right time, or putting the timer on your kitchen counter so the cookies don't burn.

In addition, you'll be able to schedule shopping trips for when it is convenient for you and your schedule. As soon as you retrieve an item from the "Spares Box," simply add the item to your shopping list for your next trip to the store. Having a spare on hand will keep your time and your home more organized.

As you begin to bring these precious spare items home on a regular basis, you can begin to implement the second part of this organizational principle: I call them "rubber-band babies."

A "rubber-band baby" is the last of any item in your home of which you have multiples. It is the last bottle of catsup, the last container of aspirin, the last jar of hand cream in your bathroom. These items are designated as a "rubber-band baby" by simply putting a rubber band around them. Then when you get the item out of the cupboard, you'll know it is the last one and you can immediately add it to a grocery or shopping list. This method of tracking the last items can save you time and energy because it serves as a warning that it's time to repurchase and replenish items for your home. No more emergency trips to the store. You are one step ahead of the game.

Using rubber bands is an easy system that even the youngest member of your household can understand and help with. "Mom, I just pulled out a 'rubber-band baby'" will be a welcome refrain, bringing you comfort and consolation.

So add "rubber bands" to your shopping list and have a "rubber-band baby" party. Go through each and every one of your cupboards, your pantry, and your medicine cabinets. Put a rubber band on the last of every item you have stored. You will probably discover several items of which you have only one. Put a rubber band on it anyway and add the item to your shopping list immediately. When you go shopping, buy extras of the item so that your "Spares Box" and your "rubber-band baby" system can be more and more functional.

Consider extending this principle to buying regularly used items in bulk so your shopping time can be further reduced. If you need one, buy two. If you need two, buy four. If you need four, buy more.

You might also consider buying a year's worth of non-perishable items at a time. I personally like to do this project in February after the excitement of the winter holidays is over and when my schedule is a little lighter. Out I go to shop for one year's supply of toilet paper, paper towels, shampoo, hand soap, liquid soap, laundry soap, and other non-food items that are part of my regular household needs. Buying in bulk like this helps to organize my home and allows me more time to be doing what I want instead of what I must.

So if you care, remember: "If I care, I'll keep a spare. I will use rubber bands as a reminder to be ahead and not behind in the shopping game. And when I can, I'll buy in bulk for one year's worth of non-perishable supplies."

5

Repairing and Replacing in a Timely Manner

I broke my shoelace recently. As usual, I pulled some of the good shoelace through the hole, tied a square knot, and decided it would have to do for now. Of course, I knew the knot would annoy me with those ends poking up and out. The shoelace was too short to tie comfortably, and it was likely to break again soon. But, well, it was how I faced life sometimes: leave it for later.

But is this the best way? How many broken or half-repaired items are irritating you because they need replacing or repair? Plastic weakens and tears, carpet edges fray, paint peels, and shoelaces break. They always have; they always will. So what can you do to get your life more in order and have fewer items that need your attention? May I suggest some ideas to help?

1. **Create a master list of items that need your attention.** Begin by walking around your home, opening your cupboards, and taking a stroll through your yard. Make a list of everything that needs repair or replacement. Throughout the week, keep an eye open for items to add to the list. Whether you are on your way out the door, in the middle of another project, or just too weary to think about it, take the time to add the necessary items to your "Repair/Replace It" list.

Once the master Repair/Replace It list has been completed, sit down with your family and decide which jobs on the list are an A priority, a B priority, or a C priority. It might also be a good idea to identify certain jobs that would be good projects for your children or teenagers to tackle as part of their weekly chores.

Then choose a regular time each week and select one repair job on the list; some families do this as part of their Saturday afternoon routine. Decide what needs to be done for that specific job and create a list of mini-steps. For example, perhaps it is time to replace the curtains in your living room. On your list of mini-steps you may have some of the following tasks:

- Gather tools (a tape measure, a screwdriver, a hammer, etc.)
- Take down old curtains and blinds
- Wash windows
- Measure windows
- Purchase and hang new curtain rods, curtains, and blinds

Then it is time to begin. Sometimes this will require a trip to the store. If you aren't going out just at the moment, add the needed repair item to your regular errands list. Put any parts or samples that you will need for comparison in your vehicle and note needed measurements on your errands list. If necessary, you can always buy the repair items one week and finish the job the next week.

2. **Create a clothing mending kit.** In this kit keep a pair of scissors, some needles, sundry buttons, safety pins of assorted sizes, and various colored threads. Remember, the more complete you can make the kit, the more likely it is you'll use it to repair your clothes. In addition, have a designated "mending basket" or closet shelf where members of your family can put items that need attention. You may wish to keep the basket near the phone so that when a good friend calls, you can finish some mending while you chat.

Of course, when your children are young, you will do most of the mending yourself, but as soon as they are able to write, they can learn to mend. If it is a hole in the sock, an unraveling in the sweatshirt, or a seam that is opening, you can teach them, gradually and carefully, to make these simple repairs. Not only will you save time and money, but, with practice and patience, your children will learn invaluable skills.

If other kinds of repairs are needed because of your children's activities or accidents, involve them early with the repairing process. Somehow broken treasures mended by their own hands become even more special because the toy or treasure has been made whole again by their efforts.

3. **In a sturdy container, keep a variety of glues, a glue gun, several small clamps, and a box of rubber bands.** Include glues that will attach anything to anything, and glues for paper, wood, and plastic surfaces. Having the necessary glues and clamping tools easily accessible will make it even easier to do the repair.

Remember, it is usually easier and faster to repair something earlier than later. This was vividly demonstrated to me when once I failed to patch a small, open seam in my hall carpet. As I vacuumed over it week after week, I noticed that small opening and ignored it. Then one day, one of my children pulled a toy over the opening. Something caught and the small opening became a "You Cannot Ignore This" rip.

So commit to a repair-it-or-replace-it mentality and feel the freedom of saying, "It's fixed!"

6

Organizing Cleaning Supplies

I don't like to clean, and I don't know many people who do. However, since cleaning will always need to be done, either by ourselves, our family, or a cleaning crew, it is essential to have the proper cleaning supplies stored, organized, and readily available upon demand.

Most of us keep our cleaning supplies in a single closet, usually one that has deep shelves, and which is overloaded with too much of too many kinds of cleaning supplies, with everything mixed up and messy.

There are several steps to organize cleaning supplies that will help make our cleaning days easier.

1. **Gather tools to help you in your organization work.** You will need:

- Several large plastic containers for organizing and sorting similar cleaning supplies
- A wastebasket
- Labels or stickers and a permanent marker to label containers

2. **Empty the closet or cupboard shelf by shelf and take an inventory of your supplies.** You may find that you have several different brands of window cleaning solutions, cleansers, toilet bowl cleaners, and

furniture polish. You may also find several partially used bottles of various cleansers. Group these duplicate items together in the plastic buckets, like supplies with like.

3. **Evaluate each type of cleaning supply** and throw away those that you haven't used for some time, don't really meet your needs, or are otherwise useless.

4. **Label the plastic buckets on the front and back.** Labeling both sides will help keep the supplies organized when they are returned to the closet.

5. **Wipe down the shelves and walls of the closet or cupboard** in order to start fresh and clean again.

6. **Return the containers of cleaning supplies back to the closet.**

It is also a good idea to have duplicate cleaning supply closets on each level of your home. While we want to get our exercise, we usually don't go to the trouble to go up- or downstairs just to get our cleaning supplies. Keeping supplies on each level will make it more convenient to clean. Remember to label the containers of cleaning supplies "UP-STAIRS" or "DOWN-STAIRS" to help the supplies be returned to their rightful homes.

Another way to organize your cleaning supplies is to create bathroom cleaning kits. In addition to storing cleaning supplies in the same container in a closet, put bathroom cleaning supplies in several plastic tote trays (I like the ones with handles best), and store one "kit" in each bathroom (be sure to keep them out of reach of small children). Because convenience is one key to finishing cleaning jobs in a timely manner, these kits will come in handy for all your cleaning jobs.

Finally, keep fewer kinds of cleaning supplies. I am surprised at how many people try a product, don't like it, but instead of throwing it away, they keep it in their cleaning supply closet and buy another product instead. Choose the best products you can afford, use them until they are gone, discard the ones that don't work, and keep the number of cleaning supplies at a minimum.

Occasionally organizing your cleaning supplies will make your housework easier to complete and will accelerate your whole housekeeping process because you have a neat, clean closet from which to retrieve the needed supplies with ease and kits to tidy the bathroom at a moment's notice.

7

The Wonder of Wastebaskets

My mom called them garbage cans. My dad called them trash cans. My husband calls them wastebaskets. But whatever you call them, they are wonderful additions to *all* the rooms in your home. Here are some tips on how to make your wastebaskets work for you.

1. **Have a wastebasket in every room in the house.** When something is handy and convenient, you tend to take advantage of it and things get done. I once worked with a woman who struggled with order in her bedroom, the only room in her shared duplex that she could call her own. As we worked through the stacks and stacks of clothing, papers, and other articles lining her walls and floor, it occurred to me that there was no wastebasket in her bedroom. She had bits of trash tucked behind the bookshelf, stuffed under her bed, and stacked on the already full desk. The nearest wastebasket was in the adjacent bathroom and it was much too small (you know the popular kind that are short and beautiful, but can't hold much more than a Q-tip and a single piece of tissue). I encouraged the woman to buy a reasonably tall, large plastic wastebasket for her personal space right away.

Each and every room in your home needs its own wastebasket, the bigger the better. (Of course, if you have young children, the wastebaskets will need to find homes up and away from their curious fingers. Otherwise, you will spend hours . . . well, you know how it can be when a child finds a wastebasket.)

2. **Replace all torn, broken, rusted, and unsightly wastebaskets.** Surprisingly, many of us keep wastebaskets long past their useful life. For some reason, even when the plastic begins to tear around the upper rim of the wastebasket, we still keep using it until the tear widens, making it difficult—and sometimes dangerous—to transport. Usually, at that point, we delay moving it and thus it gets heavier before it gets emptied and the problem compounds. Or we have a wastebasket that is rusting but still useful. We look at the rusted can every time we deposit trash and think momentarily about how old it is, but still it sits in our garage or our home. As part of your wastebasket inventory, identify those that are torn or broken or old and replace them as soon as your budget will allow.

When you are replacing wastebaskets, make sure to choose ones that are sturdy and neutral in color. Avoid buying white wastebaskets because they look dirty almost immediately. A good friend once commented to me, "Marie, you like to buy things that already look dirty so they don't look dirty when they get that way."

3. **All household wastebaskets—except for kitchen wastebaskets—should be big enough to hold a week's worth of trash.** Having a wastebasket large enough to hold a week's worth of trash means that you'll need to empty them only once a week—usually the night before or the day of your neighborhood's trash pickup. The less time you have to worry about emptying the trash means you'll have more time for other things.

4. **The kitchen wastebasket should hold at least one day's trash and be emptied daily.** The kitchen produces most of the trash in the home, so it is essential that you have a efficient system in place for gathering and removing trash. You may wish to have two kitchen wastebaskets: one for "dry" items (cereal boxes, capped and empty gallon milk jugs, the daily junk mail) and another for "wet" items (empty soup cans, orange peels, egg shells). How ever many wastebaskets you decide to have in your kitchen, keep them accessible and convenient. Ask your best

worker to be in charge of emptying the kitchen wastebaskets daily to keep the room neat and clean.

5. **Make it easy to empty household trash into the exterior garbage can.** Having all the wastebaskets in the world won't help if the trash you've gathered sits in your house instead of making its way to the exterior can for pickup. Teach your children to finish the trash-collecting chore by taking the bag to the main garbage can. You can offer incentives (treats or extra privileges) to your children when they empty the trash in the outside garbage can without being reminded.

You may also wish to move the outside garbage can inside the garage during the cold winter months to keep it from freezing shut and getting snowed upon, and also to make it easier for your family to utilize.

6. **Have a semiannual wastebasket cleaning party on a sunny day.** Take the empty plastic wastebaskets to the back lawn or patio area, spray them down, soak them for twenty minutes in soapy water, and scrub them with a brush. Tip the water out onto a safe place, let the wastebaskets sit in the sun for a few minutes to dry, then wipe them down and return them to their rooms. There is nothing quite as nice as being able to look at the bottom of a wastebasket without having to grimace at what is stuck there.

You will find these wonderful secrets of wastebasket organization are well worth the time to implement in your own home.

8

Help the Kitchen Help You

When you organize (or reorganize) the kitchen, you need to start with a master plan that will meet your needs to use throughout the project. I recommend drafting this plan on paper before you begin to move things around in the kitchen, move things out of the kitchen, and discard some things altogether.

Kitchen cupboards and drawers are meant to be helpful, but they often seem to hinder. Sometimes it is because they are simply too full, either with too many useful items or items that are out of place and should be kept elsewhere. So it's time to help the kitchen help you.

May I suggest a peaceful morning (if such an event is possible in your home), as you will need the quiet to help you concentrate on the big picture of your kitchen organization and to think through your current situation, your needs, and the master plan you will use to begin your work. For our purposes, we are going to suppose you can't make major remodeling changes to your kitchen and your main purpose is simply to organize your kitchen so it will be more effective and useful to you.

Gather several sheets of paper (lined paper or graph paper might be a good choice since we will be making several lists) and clip the paper to a sturdy writing surface, like a clipboard, or clear the surface of the table so you have plenty of room to work. Then open all your kitchen cupboards so you can see into them. Sit comfortably away from this scene and for a few minutes simply look at what you see. Observe, ponder, and ask yourself some questions: Why is that item stored there? Why are there so many of those utensils? Why aren't there enough of these tools? Why is that item in the kitchen at all?

Label the top of three sheets of paper with one of these three headings: "Discard," "Keep," and "Move." Divide each paper into two main columns. As you examine your cupboards and drawers, list each item in the left-hand column of one of these three categories. You may find it easier at this stage of the process to list groups of items instead of individual items. For example, under the "Keep" heading you may have "pots and pans" or "measuring cups and spoons." Under the "Discard" heading you may list "mismatched plastic containers and lids." For each item on the "Move" list, jot down in the right-hand column where the item belongs instead.

Now it's time to decide where to put what. Items in the kitchen should be stored using the A-B-C process. Items that are frequently used—the "A" items—should be stored in "A" places. These are the areas in your kitchen where you can reach with minimal bending down or stretching up. The top drawers under the counters, the bottom shelf of your upper cupboards, and the front area of your lower cupboards are examples of "A" storage areas.

The goal is to make the process of retrieving utensils and tools during your time in the kitchen a "one-handed" motion. Because one hand is usually dirty or wet while cooking, we often have only one hand to get out a knife, or bring down a bowl, or retrieve a pan.

Keep only the essential "A" tools such as spatulas, stirring spoons, peelers, scissors, and knives in the top drawers of your lower cabinets. Most kitchens need only a few tools in an "A" drawer and these should be the ones you use all the time. Store other tools and specialty items that are needed but used less frequently in lower drawers or other places.

Items that are used less often go in "B" places. These are drawers and shelves where you have to stretch up or kneel down to reach them. Items that are rarely used can go in "C" places: the rear of the shelves, the lowest or highest cupboard shelves, and the deep corner cupboards.

Review your "Keep" list and write down either "A," "B," or "C" next to each item.

You may find that you require multiples of some tools. For instance, if you are always retrieving measuring cups or spoons from the dishwasher, you may want to consider keeping multiple sets on hand in order to have a clean set ready to use at all times. It is helpful to have multiple sets of cutting boards, whisks, spatulas, and mixing spoons as well.

In the right-hand column of your "Keep" list, make a notation next to any items that you need multiples of. You can transfer the notes to your grocery shopping list to use the next time you are at the store. Likewise, you may notice some items that you have too many of. Mark those items as duplicates and list the extra items on your "Discard" list.

DISCARD		KEEP		MOVE	
mismatched plastic containers and lids	→ throw away	pots and pans	C	toys	→ playroom
		measuring cups and spoons	A (stack by size)	phone books	→ home office
extra steak knives	→ donate	cookie sheets	B (buy multiples)	sport bag	→ garage

In addition, consider "unstacking" items that are not the same size, such as mixing bowls or plastic containers. It seems that we always need the item at the bottom of the stack, and it's often inconvenient to sort through a stack of bowls or pans to retrieve the one we want. So "unstack unlikes." Have a separate stack for large plates, small plates, and cereal bowls. Likewise, "stack alikes." Items that are the same shape and purpose can be stacked, such as mixing bowls of the same size, storage containers, or plastic drinking glasses.

The average stove has only four elements, so unstack your pans and store your favorite four pans with their lids in an "A" place and put less-used pans in a "B" or "C" place in your cupboards.

Take a moment to review your "Keep" list and make a note in the right-hand column next to any items that would be good candidates to reorganize into stacks by size and likeness.

There might be "maybes" in your kitchen and on your list. These are items you are not really sure about. Maybe you really need them. Maybe you don't. Maybe they don't belong anywhere else, but you're not sure if you should discard them yet. It is best to put these items in a box labeled "Kitchen Maybes" and store it a nearby closet or the garage. During the next few weeks, retrieve any items you really need and find room for them in the "A" or "B" spaces of your kitchen. Whatever is left in the box after a two-week period can be stored in the "C" areas. An even better idea would be to simply donate them or discard them with the other items on your "Discard" list.

Kitchen cupboards are meant to keep kitchen tools convenient and orderly. If something is clogging the process, getting in the way, or just taking up space—get rid of it!

So look for a free half-hour, gather paper, a pen, and a sturdy writing surface and begin planning.

Once you have your plan in hand and you know on paper where everything is going to go, you are ready to implement it. Physically moving the items around in your kitchen may take some time, so don't try to accomplish the planning and the moving in one morning or even one day. Break up your master plan into small steps and work on it in small stages. Perhaps you have an hour one day that you can focus on gathering up the items on your "Discard" list. Take a few minutes another day to unstack and restack your stacks. Make a trip to the store to buy dividers for your drawers, containers for your utensils, and labels for your shelves and cupboards.

Your kitchen is a busy place; don't make it harder on yourself by emptying out your cupboards and drawers only to have to leave it half-done to make dinner. Try, instead, to complete small portions of this bigger project whenever possible.

Cleaning out and organizing the items in your kitchen cupboards will significantly contribute to your kitchen's well-being and make cooking a simpler and more pleasant daily task.

9

Tackling Problem Pantries

Kitchen pantries can make your home management experience a dream or they can turn into a recurring nightmare. You may be blessed with a pantry that has ample room, plenty of storage space, and lots of shelves that are just the right height, depth, and width. Or you may be maintaining a pantry in the end cupboards of your small apartment kitchen. No matter your circumstances, though, there are certain principles that will make your pantry work better each and every day.

1. **Set aside thirty minutes or so of uninterrupted time to organize your pantry.**

Start by clearing and wiping off your kitchen counters and table. Pull everything out of the pantry (yes, everything) and place the items in stacks on your kitchen counters and table. Group items of similar types together as much as possible: the cold cereals, the chips, the canned goods, the pastas, the bottles, and the soda cans. As you are grouping and sorting, take a moment to check the expiration dates on your items. Throw away anything that is past its prime.

2. **Wipe down all the pantry shelving, top to bottom.** Sweep and mop the floor. After all, if you are going to have an organized pantry, you might as well have a clean one, too.

3. **Sort the items from your pantry using the following guidelines:**

Organize your pantry items using the A-B-C storage method. Items that are used most frequently are "A" items and should be stored on the shelves you can reach without stretching up or bending down. Items that are used infrequently are "B" items and should be stored in the areas that are less accessible (meaning places where you have to stretch or bend to reach). Items that are rarely used are "C" items and should be stored in the least accessible areas: the upper shelves (those you can reach only by using a stool or chair) and any back corners.

Reserve the "A" shelves and areas of your pantry for the "in and out" items. These are for foods that are frequently used or retrieved: cold cereal, chips for school lunches, or raisins for afternoon snacks. It is important to reserve space for these foods whether or not you currently have them in stock in the pantry. You may even want to label the shelves: cold cereal, lunch foods, and afternoon snacks.

It may sound like a lot of wasted space, but the trouble with over-stuffed pantries is that you have to remove half the stuff to get at what you want. It is better to "under" store the pantry in order to make retrieving items more convenient than to "over" store and make a mess every time you open the pantry door.

Return to the pantry only items that logically belong there. Often items are initially placed in the pantry because it was convenient: "I'll put this here for now." As you organize, do not return any items to your pantry unless that is its proper home. Set aside the orphans for placement in other cupboards and closets of your home, but don't spend time now actually putting them away. Stay focused on the project at hand!

As you return items to the pantry, remember to keep like items with like items as much possible. This means keeping all the cold cereals together, all the pastas together, and all the instant puddings together. Oversized plastic containers can be helpful in keeping like items together. When you need the chips, for example, out comes the "chips" container.

It is also helpful to put specific like items *behind* specific like items.

In other words, if you have a dozen cans of tomato soup, stack them one on top of the other and one behind the other on the same shelf.

As much as possible, store items that belong in the same "like family" next to each other on the shelves. For instance, you may have several cans of a variety of soups—chicken noodle, tomato, vegetable beef— so group the chicken noodle soup one behind the other and *next to* the tomato which is *next to* the vegetable beef.

A pantry is a high-maintenance creature. If you neglect it, it will come back to haunt you every time you open the door. So, now that you understand the methods for making your pantry more functional, set up a maintenance schedule and stick to it. Many home managers find that a quick "spiff up" before they go grocery shopping each week works well. You not only immediately see what needs replenishing, but then when you have finished shopping, you can restore order to the pantry as you restock the shelves, moving the soup can back to its rightful place and straightening the cereal boxes so they are organized again.

Someday all kitchens will have adequate and roomy pantries, but for now, no matter your pantry situation, clean it out, organize the items as you return them to the pantry, and see what a wonderful difference having a pantry partner can be in your kitchen life!

10

Spice Cabinet Savvy

Spices easily clutter our cupboards. It is time to decide, to divide, and to discard. It is time to take control! And our first step is to identify the types of spices in our cupboards. You can usually divide your spices into five different categories:

1. **The "A" spices are the ones we use all the time** in our main meal preparation. They usually include salt, pepper, seasoned salt, minced onions, garlic powder, and any others that you find yourself using at almost every session at the stove.

These "A" spices should be right up front and close to the stove so they can be easily reached as you are preparing meals. I like to keep these spices alphabetized on a round turntable so they can be retrieved with a simple twist of the wrist, and returned after use just as easily.

2. **The "B" spices are those we use when we are baking** and include baking soda, baking powder, cocoa, cinnamon, salt (again), and other common spices you like to use to make a delicious dessert.

These "B" spices are best kept near the mixing counter so they will be readily available as the dessert is being prepared. If you have room on your kitchen counter, a second spice turntable is a useful choice, otherwise you can store these spices in a small box or container. Unless the kitchen is unusually small, or the stove and mixing center are next to each other, you may want to consider having duplicate salt containers, one for each location, to save steps when you work in the kitchen.

3. **The "C" spices are often exotic spices** we have little use for in daily meal preparation but which we plan to use occasionally when trying out a new recipe. These spices often spend more time cluttering our cupboards than flavoring our meals.

These "C" spices are best stored away from the main area of the kitchen. I suggest putting them in a shallow container—a labeled shoebox will work—in a remote corner of a kitchen cupboard. That way they are available when we need them, but they are not cluttering up the precious workspace of the central areas of the kitchen.

4. **The "D" spices are the spare spices:** the second bottle of minced onions you got on sale, the extra bottle of cinnamon that you bought when you thought you were out. You know you will need them eventually, so you want to keep them, but you don't want them cluttering up the kitchen until then.

Store these "D" spices in a more isolated spot, such as with your other food storage items or in a bottom corner of your pantry, but make sure to label them and keep them together so that finding and retrieving them is effortless. It also makes it easier for you to know if you have completely run out of a spice or if you simply need to move the duplicate spice from its storage area to the kitchen.

5. **The "E" spices are the dregs of our spice cabinet:** those we have inherited, those we purchased on a whim but have never used, and those we hold on to for some reason, even though we have no idea when or how to use them. (How should cardamom be used, anyway?)

These "E" spices should be kept in a convenient spot: the wastebasket! You can always buy turmeric again if you really need it. Just because you bought it doesn't mean you have to keep it until it is all gone. Sometimes we just have to chalk our mistakes up to experience and rid our lives of the little items that make our kitchen unworkable, messy, and otherwise burdensome. Out, out, out go those unwanted, unneeded, and unused spices! (Or you could donate them to a friend who likes to experiment with recipes and exotic cooking.)

So take at a look at your spice situation. Pull all the spices out of your cupboards and sort them into five groups: "A" (cooking), "B" (baking), "C" (exotic), "D" (extra), and "E" (disposable).

Return the "A" spices to a place near the stove, put the "B" spices close to your mixing center, find an out-of-the-way place for your "C" spices, find a convenient storage spot for your "D" spices, and bravely separate yourself from your "E" spices.

Having a trim and slim spice collection makes any cook more willing to be in the kitchen!

11

Junk the Junk Drawer

W e all have one. The one drawer in the kitchen jammed with tools, paper, pens, and odds and ends of every description: the infamous "junk drawer." It's time to dump the junk and organize the drawer into something more useful: a kitchen home tool drawer.

It seems that when we keep all our tools strictly in the garage, we spend innumerable hours before starting a home repair project simply looking for items that have been misplaced, lent out, or are hidden from our view. Having an indoor tool collection is an excellent way to organize your home and save you time.

To begin the transformation of your junk drawer, spread a large, old bath towel on the table or counter to catch the lint as well as to protect and keep the counter clean. Set out three shoeboxes or plastic containers next to the wastebasket. As you sort through the items from your junk drawer, simply toss in the trash the items you never use, that are broken, or that are missing pieces. Gather the items that logically belong in the garage into one box. Items that belong in another part of the house go into another box. And items that you wish to keep in the kitchen drawer go into a third box.

You may wish to further sort the items from the third box into two additional categories. "Hardware and tools" would include the stray nails, screws, batteries, scissors, and the like that will form the core of your new tool drawer. "Business materials and supplies" would include the pens, pencils, paper clips, notepaper, and coupons that seem to be ever-present in a junk drawer. It is a good idea to store these items in two separate drawers so you don't have to rummage through sharp nails and heavy hammers to find a pen that works or a piece of paper to take down a phone message.

When you are ready to assemble your kitchen tool drawer, arrange your drawer dividers to keep small items confined and larger items lined up with each other. You can find drawer dividers at almost any grocery store or home furnishing store. Sometimes even an extra plastic silverware separator tray can suit your purposes.

After you have found or purchased dividers that work for you and have placed them in the drawer, use sponges or rolled towels to anchor and secure the dividers so they will not move as the drawer is opened and closed. This small trick will help keep the home tool drawer more organized with less hassle.

So what tools should be in this drawer in order to ease the maintenance and repair of your home?

A good kitchen tool kit should include:

- A hammer (for driving nails when hanging pictures)
- A screwdriver (I like the four-in-one kind that has four different, interchangeable heads)
- A screw starter (a small, screwdriver-like tool with a pointed, rounded, grooved tip for making an easy pre-entry hole in a wall or piece of wood to enable the screw to go in straight)
- A flat razor with a sturdy handle (for carefully cleaning fly specks off windows or scraping dried jam from floors)
- A heavy-duty cutting razor (for breaking down boxes)
- A tape measure
- A pair of pliers
- A flashlight

- A small container of spare screws, nails, and other miscellaneous hardware, which will make setting up and maintaining a home easier

ROLLED TOWEL			
ITEMS IN A DIVIDER			
ITEMS IN A DIVIDER	ITEMS IN A DIVIDER	ITEMS IN A DIVIDER	SPONGE

DRAWER FRONT

To this supply of tools, you might also want to add a good, reusable paint brush, a supply of Velcro strips, plastic ties, or other items that you frequently use. Remember, have what you need for the *inside* of the house, *inside* the house. It will make all the difference in how you cope with making repairs, decorating, and fixing things.

12

Laundry Room Layout

I have seen time and again how important it is to set up a room properly in order to get the job done right. This is especially true of the laundry room. Whether your laundry room is a designated area of the garage, an unfinished area of your basement, or a furnished room in your home, it is important to set up your laundry room properly to expedite the laundry. You see, laundry is never-ending. We will wash the same clothes and towels over and over, so why not take a few minutes to set up the laundry room with the right tools and supplies in order to make the whole process easier. How is it possible? Here are four simple ideas that will make your laundry day a breeze.

1. **Store the laundry soap (granulated or liquid) next to the washing machine.** It sounds like a basic idea, but storing granulated soap at the same level as the washing machine makes scooping the soap into the washer easy and convenient with very little mess or spillage. If you stack three 40-pound soap buckets on top of each other, the top bucket will be at the same level as your washer.

If you use liquid soap, it is easy to store the soap in a cupboard or on a shelf above the washer, then simply tip the container forward, pull open the spout to pour the liquid into the washer, and then push the container back into its storage area.

2. **Put a wastebasket next to the dryer for lint disposal.** If you position a small wastebasket close to the dryer door, you can collect the lint quickly and deposit it directly in the wastebasket, saving time and keeping the lint dust to a minimum, thereby keeping the room cleaner.

3. **Prepare a place to put the clothes when they are dried.** Every organized laundry room should have a folding table and a clothing rod with plenty of standardized hangers. These items will help make doing the laundry quick and easy.

A clothing rod is useful for those clothing items that must be line dried or for clothes that need to be hung up immediately out of the dryer to avoid wrinkling. A simple way to install a clothing rod is to use a standard tension shower rod between two walls. You can also hang up a curtain rod by screwing two hooks into the ceiling and attaching a short length of chain.

Next, get rid of all those various-sized metal hangers you might have inherited from the dry cleaners, the hangers that came with clothing purchases, and any other odd-sized hangers that are old, weak, or misshapen. Using standardized plastic or wood hangers is a great way to keep your laundry organized and under control. You may even wish to assign a specific color of hanger to individuals in your family to help make sure the right clothes go back to the right room.

Finally, set up a "folding table" near the dryer. Use a small table, install a countertop, or even simply cover some stacked boxes with a blanket. This table doesn't have to be expensive or even purchased at a store to get the job done. It just needs to be convenient so you can easily sort and fold the laundry after it is dried.

4. **Place a laundry basket or container in every bedroom and bathroom in the house.** This can save you time and trouble. Not only will all the bathroom towels already be gathered in one basket, but assigning a laundry basket to a room means that you can use the same basket to transport the dirty clothes to the laundry room and the clean clothes back again. The baskets are collected full of dirty laundry from each room,

the wash is done, the clean items are folded, stacked, and returned to these same baskets. After the laundry has been put away, the baskets are already in place to collect another round of dirty clothes.

It is important to teach your family that a basket of laundry isn't "done" until the clothes are hung up in the closet or folded in dresser drawers. When your family members help out by putting away their clothes in a timely manner, it cuts a big job down to a manageable size.

Doing laundry will never be done (although it can be finished for the day). And it may never even be pleasant, but there are things you can do to set up the laundry room to make doing the laundry easier and to let you spend your time on other, nicer tasks.

13

Laundry: Marathon or Sprint?

Should laundry be handled in day-long marathons of work once a week, or a daily quick sprint of one or two loads? It's a question that needs answering as we approach trying to organize a consistent irritant in life: the laundry.

Surely laundry is a life-long, never-ending, always-present, never-will-go-away marathon. But it can be handled, tamed, and organized in small steps and quick sprints.

First of all, I don't recommend routinely doing a marathon laundry session. I know some people who manage to do all their laundry on Mondays and are finished with it for the week, but most of us have more complex schedules than that and if Monday comes and we don't get to the laundry, then we are faced with two weeks of laundry the next Monday. Instead, plan to do laundry every day. For example:

- Monday: two batches of weekend clothes
- Tuesday: one batch of bath towels
- Wednesday: two batches of weekday clothes
- Thursday: one batch of sheets
- Friday: two batches of weekday clothes

When you do laundry every day, you can involve everyone in the family and let everyone make a contribution, however small. Suzie can fold and put away the kitchen towels on Tuesday; Mike and John can strip their bed sheets and bring them to the laundry room on Thursday morning; everyone can put their clothes away after they have been washed and folded on Monday, Wednesday, and Friday. Your honey can put his or her own work clothes in the washer on Saturday morning and begin the load.

I have found that the best way to run the ongoing laundry marathon is to always have the washer running while you are doing something else. Buy a small pocket timer. When you start a batch of wash, set the timer for the length of the washer cycle. Keep the timer in your pocket as you go about your other daily chores or activities. When the timer buzzes, you'll know it is time to return to the laundry room and move the washed clothes to the dryer, the dry clothes to the folding table, the folded clothes to a basket, and the basket back upstairs. Start a new batch of wash and set the timer again. You'll be amazed at how efficiently you can process several loads of laundry simply by making laundry part of your daily dance, not an interruption to it.

You can also use the timer as a motivator for your children to put their laundry away. Make it a race and see who finishes first. Or see if your child can beat yesterday's time. A well-used timer can be a fun and valuable way to keep the laundry under control.

Another way to help you organize your laundry is to reduce the size of your family's wardrobe and eliminate the clothes that are old, worn, torn, or that no longer fit or are no longer in style.

While each family will have to decide their own standards, a good rule of thumb is to have five core tops and five bottoms for children under twelve, ten core tops and five bottoms for teens until they are grown, and ten core tops and ten bottoms for yourself and your husband (along with a few mix and match items for variety and special occasions). Add a sweater, light jacket, and heavier coat (along with mittens, hat, and scarf for wintertime fun), and your family will have a practical and functional wardrobe that will be easy to maintain and launder.

If you have a family with young children, consider carefully before buying white shirts (except boy's and men's white dress shirts, of course). No matter how careful you are, white shirts will never be white again. Ever. There will be mustard, catsup, dirt, and chocolate to stain those beautiful white clothes. Yes, bleach can clean a lot of things, but why complicate your life when the possibility of ruining a new white shirt with a chocolate ice cream cone is a high probability? Keep to darker neutrals, patterns, and heavier fabrics until your family is grown (or old enough to do their own laundry) to save yourself a lot of laundry time.

Perhaps the only exception to this rule is white socks. Buying the same brand and style of white socks will help cut down on the time it takes to match and roll socks for your family.

Take a few minutes each day to do your laundry and to sort through your family's clothes to identify the clothes you can store until next season, donate, or discard. As you pace yourself through the laundry marathon and reduce your family's wardrobe, you'll find you have more energy and time for other activities.

14

Organizing the Garage

I s your garage messy? For most people the garage is the one area of the house that is often neglected or ignored, left to be dealt with "someday." However, an organized garage can facilitate so much efficiency into a family's life that organizing it should be a high priority.

Why does the garage get messy, anyway? For many of us it is the "halfway house" to the garbage can. We no longer want a specific item, but we are not quite brave enough to discard it outright. So we move it to the garage and leave it to "season" for a while. Other times we know an item doesn't belong in the kitchen, bedroom, or basement, but don't know where else to put it. So into the garage it goes.

Many times our garage is messy because family members neglect putting away what they get out. The shovel is laid against the wall and slowly slides down until it is in our path. The children's bikes are in a tangled heap because the bikes were not returned to their designated places after a Saturday ride.

It's even possible you might never have gotten the garage organized in the first place when you originally moved into your home. That could be anywhere from two months to eight years ago. It is hard to keep organized what didn't start out that way!

But with some time, some planning, and some work, we can get the garage functioning and capable of being a nice room to drive into after a long trip, a day away, or just when you return from errands.

Just as in cleaning and organizing the kitchen, it is important to divide the project into several small steps. Don't try to do everything in one afternoon; plan first, then execute.

Before you even begin to do the actual work of physically organizing the garage, take a moment to organize it mentally. Make a list of your needs, desires, and capacities. There are several important decisions that will need to be made about how to utilize the space in your garage. Here are three common kinds of garage storage:

- Hang it (from overhead rafters or joists)
- Shelve it (along the walls)
- Stack it (in plastic tubs or sturdy produce boxes)

You may decide the best way to organize the bikes is to install bike hooks and hang them from the rafters. You may want your spouse to drill holes in the handles of the garden tools and to hang them along the wall. You may have a long back wall that would be perfect to stack boxes or install shelving. Write down what you will need to buy or gather—whether it is bike hooks, drill bits, nails, boxes, or labels. This thinking work, done before the actual cleaning and setting up of the garage, will make the process easier and faster. The end result will be an area that will be easy to maintain day after day, month after month.

After making your decisions, a thorough cleanup is in order. Choose a warm day when you'll have time to focus on the garage. Begin by sweeping off the driveway and designating three specific sorting areas: "Keep," "Maybe," and "Toss." As you move all the items out of the garage, place them in one of these three areas.

The items in the Keep pile will eventually be returned to the garage; the items in the Toss pile should be either tossed out or donated. (Try your best to make the Toss pile your largest one.)

The items in the Maybe pile are set aside so you can reconsider them one more time after your initial sort. Sometimes the second time around we are braver about what to keep and what to throw away: "Yes, let's keep the extra cooler until our children are grown." "No, we don't need the scooter. No one has ridden it for three years. Let's give it away." "Yes, let's keep three of the hoes, but we can throw those two rusted ones away."

Once the Maybe pile has been completely sorted through a second time, it is time to resort the remaining Keep items into general groups according to use. For instance, you may have one or more of the following categories:

- Bikes, scooters, skateboards
- Sports equipment
- Garden tools and supplies
- Woodworking tools
- Camping gear
- Automotive tools

Review your plan that lists where you have decided to store each of these groups of items: "We will hang the bikes from the rafters, store the camping equipment on one side wall, hang the gardening equipment on the back wall, and put the sports equipment boxed on the second side wall." Then, before you move anything back into the garage, install the bike hooks, drill holes in the garden tools, and box up the sports equipment.

If you are storing smaller items in larger containers, label both sides of the container in large and legible handwriting to help you identify and retrieve the right carton during your next visit to the garage.

Remember, in order for your garage to work effectively there should be about three feet free to either side of the vehicles when they are parked in the garage, about six-and-one-half feet overhead clearance, about one foot in front of each vehicle, and about two feet behind each vehicle.

Cleaning out and organizing the garage can be a major project for most people, so make sure to divide the work into small sections. Take a few minutes one day to implement the Keep, Maybe, and Toss principles to one small section of the garage. And then do it again on another day. Then when you are ready to clean out the entire garage, you will have already made many decisions that will make the final process faster and easier.

Once it is finished, the garage becomes a convenient and accessible storage area. An organized garage helps any family function at a higher level.

15

Your Home Office: Command Central

Where do you start to make that abode of yours more manageable when you first desire to get organized? Setting up a home office is a great place to begin. Why? Because dealing with the constant chaos of too many unorganized papers causes enormous stress. On the other hand, sorting, confining, and managing paperwork brings a great sense of control to a home manager's life.

So let's set up a home office. There are several essentials we will need:

- A flat surface upon which to work (the bigger the better)
- A small drawer or container for office supplies and tools
- A larger drawer or box for filing papers (which will help confine and conquer the paperwork)

First, while an actual desk with small and large drawers is best, almost any flat surface may be used—your kitchen table, a card table in a corner of a bedroom, even a slab of wood supported by two crates and covered with a tablecloth. Remember, the most important thing is that the surface should be kept reasonably clear and ready for your use at all times. Paperwork is best handled without first having to clean up a previous mess.

Likewise, a comfortable desk chair is a nice addition to a home office, but it need not be fancy or fine, just easy to sit on, sturdy to use, and convenient to your desk. Good lighting, a corkboard, a phone, and some shelving can complete a home office's organizational setup.

Second, prepare a small container or drawer for your office supplies. Gather or purchase tools that will aid you in handling paperwork: paper clips, a stapler, a three-hole punch, scissors, pencils and pens, Post-it notes, and Scotch tape. Keep these items together and as close as possible to the desk so you can work as soon as you have a chance to sit down and focus.

Some home managers have found it useful to label these home office tools with their name so when they are borrowed, they will be easy to identify and return.

Third, designate a larger desk drawer or a convenient, sturdy box to hold file folders. Four file folders should be labeled immediately: "To Do," "Pending," "Bills to Pay," and "To File." Every piece of personal mail or paperwork that comes into the home should be kept in one of these folders until it can be handled and resolved.

Papers in the "To Do" file are dealt with first every time you tackle paperwork. This chore should be regularly scheduled into your daily housekeeping plan.

Papers in the "Pending" file have been partially handled but are awaiting some kind of follow-up: a reply (rebates), an event (a wedding), or a response (from someone you have written or called).

"Bills to Pay" is self-explanatory. This file keeps the unpaid bills in one place until they can be paid in a timely manner. It is helpful to jot down a reminder on your calendar of anything time-sensitive so you do not miss an important due date or deadline.

The "To File" folder is where papers of value are kept for one month before being re-examined to see if they really are worth keeping in a long-term, permanent filing cabinet or box.

It might also be helpful to have a small shredder next to your office wastebasket so you can quickly and conveniently shred any personal documents for your protection.

Another good idea is to have stackable letter trays for each family member, labeled, and stacked on the home office desk. Children and your spouse can put paperwork in Mother's letter tray when it needs her attention; she puts their paperwork, mail, and other personal papers in their slots as needed. Phone messages, magazines, and other mail can be sorted and have an immediate home as soon as these items enter the house.

It is also a good idea to create a permanent home for papers you refer to repeatedly, such as the soccer schedule, the calendar for school holidays, and the school class schedule for your teenagers. A sturdy, three-ring binder—your "Information Binder"—with tabbed binder dividers labeled for each family member makes a convenient place to keep important papers close at hand for easy access and referral. When the next important schedule comes home, transfer any necessary dates to the family calendar, then file the original in its proper place in the "Information Binder."

With the acquisition of these few tools—a flat surface, a small container for office supply tools, and a larger container for file folders—you can set up a home office. With some practice and a system to suit your personality and time constraints, you can readily handle paperwork with ease, sorting and arranging it until it becomes second nature. So set up a system that works for your family and establish a routine for handling paperwork, and you will be ready to be a professional home manager with your own home office.

16

A Best-Price Box

What is the best way to begin saving more money with everyday purchases? Experience has taught me it is best to set up a system to track your own "best prices." The knowledgeable consumer knows what a good price is on an item no matter what the ad, the sale, the placement of the item in the store, or the allure of the aisle display case. You can make all future purchases with reassurance if you create your own "Best-Price Box" and keep it up to date.

The Best-Price Box allows you to easily keep track of prices for food and non-food items that you regularly purchase. You will need a set of alphabetical (A-Z) index card dividers, 200 or so lined 3" x 5" index cards, and a recipe card box with a good clasp.

Begin by drawing six columns on one lined index card, labeled with the headings: item, brand, size, price, store, and date. This is your master index card and should be placed in the front of the index card box as a reminder for what each column stands for. Then draw six columns on the rest of the index cards and store them in the back of the box. You are now ready to begin filling up your Best-Price Box with information.

For instance, you see a good sale on paper towels at Sam's Grocery. Fifty square feet is selling for $.65. Enter the information on your index card as follows: (item) paper towels, (brand) Brawny, (size) 50 sq. ft., (cost) $.65, (store) S (use abbreviations to save time and space), and (date) 04/01.

ITEM	BRAND	SIZE	PRICE	STORE	DATE
PAPER TOWELS					
$.013/square foot	Brawny	50'	$0.65	S	04/01
$.014/square foot	R	48'	$0.68	A	02/02
DON'T BUY AGAIN - rough	WF	200'	$4.25	S	02/03
$.028/square foot	Brawny	25	$0.70	A	02/04

Each time you see a good price in an ad, a great price in the store, or make a purchase at an excellent price, note these six particulars on your cards. Then take your Best-Price Box whenever you go shopping. You will never again be caught wondering if the item in front of you is a good price or not. And the more you habitually track prices, the more you will know you are getting the best price every time.

Sometimes there will be sufficient funds in your budget to make bulk purchases at the best price. That can extend your savings even further and give you more time in your life. Other times a simple note in your records will keep you informed for the next time you make a purchase. But whether you shop a lot or a little, keep your Best-Price Box handy to help you evaluate and purchase like a pro.

We can all use some extra dollars here and there and with your Best-Price Box in hand, watch how quickly it adds up!

17

Saving Money and Getting Out of Debt

I knew of a family that was actually doing quite well with credit card debt and was only burdened with car and house payments. However, their situation always demanded they get an advance from a family friend for a week or so because the bills came due before the monthly paycheck did. While they appreciated the generosity of their friend, they knew it was time to be more financially independent. But how to begin?

It's the same with most of us. We are financially sound in some places of our lives, but would appreciate a little space between the arrival of an anticipated paycheck and the bills' due dates. How can we bring more order to our finances? What should be done and how?

First, set a goal to move from living off this month's check to living off last month's check.

Here is a five-step program you can adopt right away in order to realize this goal and organize your financial routine. It will take will power, patience, and hard work, but it will be well worth the effort.

1. **Calculate how much more money you would need in order to be one month ahead on your bills.** In the example of the family above, it would be one month's mortgage payment and one month's car payment.

2. **Write down the amount you need to save at the top of a sheet of graph paper.** Each square on the graph equals one dollar. Outline the number of squares equal to the amount of money in your goal. This represents the debt you owe yourself in order to pull ahead of your financial obligations and begin paying your debts with your own savings.

In the beginning, you may need to continue the patterns you are currently using to stay afloat, whether it is borrowing from a good friend or paying your bills as soon as your paycheck arrives. At the same time, however, you need to begin to save up money to get ahead.

3. **Review your budget to see where you might be able to make some cuts.** Could you knock $20 a week off your food budget, $10 a month off your clothing budget, and $50 a month off your spending money? If so, you'll be able to save $140 a month.

4. **Set up a new savings account.** At the end of every week transfer the money you have saved directly into the account. Let's say you decide not to eat out one week and instead save the $30. Maybe the next week you find a pair of shoes for less than you anticipated. Deposit the difference into your bank account as well. Slowly but diligently build up the amount of money you are saving in order to pay all your bills in a timely manner. For each dollar that you stash away, mark off one square on your graph chart. This will act as a visual motivator to work toward your goal.

5. **When you have saved a month's worth of money, begin paying off your bills from this new savings account.** Then, when the paychecks arrive, simply replenish your savings account and rest easy knowing you have enough set aside and are ready to pay the bills.

It may take some time to put that much money aside, and it may be hard to break some of your spending habits, but it will be well worth a small sacrifice now for the bigger benefit of being more financially independent month to month in the future.

Talk frequently with your spouse about your goal. Talk about your progress and about possible ways to save even more money. Remember to congratulate yourselves for taking the initiative to become financially independent and able to pay your debts when they come due. Make getting ahead financially a reality in your life!

ORGANIZE
YOUR FAMILY

18

Setting Up a Family Calendar

D o you want your family to be more organized and less rushed? Whether there are only two of you, or you have a large family with lots of kids, prepare and use a family calendar to have calmer days all year long.

A well-used wall calendar is an organized family's best friend. It is a tool that is best prepared diligently at the first of the year, updated each month, reviewed each week, and then looked at each and every day to do its best job.

Twelve-month wall calendars are usually available year-round at office supplies stores for a modest price. Purchase one right away to get a head start on a more organized life. Using the right tool will make your life more organized and will improve each and every day all year long.

Start by labeling the calendar with all the known events for the rest of the year. This might include business trips, birthdays, holidays, children's school and sports schedules, family reunions, and potential family vacation dates. Use colorful marking pens to emphasize important dates. Draw red hearts on Valentine's Day, add balloon stickers for birthdays, and affix shiny stars on national holidays.

You may also wish to use stickers to help your family remember the regular, repetitive events: blue stickers on Tuesdays for piano lessons, green stickers on Wednesday for football practice, and pink stickers on Friday for dance lessons. Even the youngest members of your family can easily learn to associate colored stickers with certain recurring activities.

Any time you receive an invitation to an event (such as a wedding, shower, or birthday party), note the date, time, and details on the calendar. Then file the invitation in a convenient location to use for later reference as the event draws near.

Because this wall calendar is for your whole family's use, keep it in a prominent place in your home—perhaps near the kitchen table or next to the refrigerator or in the family room.

January

		Sandwiches & football 1 all day	2	Piano lessons 3	4	Holiday décor down 5
6	7	Regular checkup 3 pm 8	Buy food for birthday 9 party	Piano lessons 10	Dad's birthday 11	12
13	Kids off school 14	15	16	Piano lessons 17	18	19
Have Grandma over for dinner 20	21	22	Visit Grandpa's grave 23	Piano lessons 24	25	Valentine's décor up 26
27	28	29	Buy Valentine cards 30	No Piano lessons 31		

At the beginning of each month, review the calendar and add additional notes and events. For every item on the calendar, ask yourself, "What does this commitment entail and how am I going to do it?" The answer will help you create smaller to-do lists that are easy to manage and schedule.

Take note of upcoming events. If Kevin's birthday is on the 15th, when will you take him birthday shopping? Make a note on the calendar. If you have a traditional family party on the 25th, when will you go to the specialty grocery store to purchase the ingredients for that special dessert? Note the date on the calendar.

At the beginning of each week, hold a short family council with everyone in your household to review the events for the upcoming week, learn about school assignments, projects, and tests (such as the important spelling bee on Friday), coordinate rides to and from various activities (such as how two parents will get four children to three different places on the same evening), plan the preparation for festivities (such as baking the cookies for the back-to-school night), and get babysitting commitments from your teenagers (so you and your spouse can have a date night out).

At the beginning of the evening meal, glance at the calendar, quickly review what is planned for tomorrow, and remind family members of their commitments and responsibilities. For instance, "George, tomorrow I will be picking you up right after school to take you to piano lessons. Would you please take the piano books to the car tonight after you practice?" "Mary, brownies need to be baked for your party tomorrow. I can help you prepare them after dinner." "Frank, when shall we fill up the sedan with gas for the weekend drive to the wedding up north?"

Remember, no matter when you start, a family calendar will help your family run smoother. Just begin now and fill out the calendar for the rest of the year, update it at the beginning of each month, discuss commitments weekly with your family, and review the calendar each evening at dinnertime. You will notice an immediate and lasting improvement in your family's everyday life.

19

Designating and Delegating Jobs

W hatever the size of your home or your family, getting help with the housework can be downright difficult at times. In fact, sometimes it's close to impossible and you end up just doing it yourself instead of struggling with trying to convince your family to help. My own experience has led me to identify four distinct personalities when it comes to getting the chores done (and sometimes one person can have multiple personalities).

Can you identify with the following types?

- The sheriff (who insists everything be fair, completely and unalterably reasonable, or they won't cooperate)
- The slacker (who doesn't like to start, works slowly and without distinction, and often has a hard time finishing a job)
- The scrimper (who gets to the job all right, but hides plenty of things under the bed or behind the door; wipes, but doesn't clean; straightens, but doesn't really do a good job)
- The complainer (who is always whining, giving excuses, or mumbling)

What can we do to reduce or eliminate the presence of these personalities in our homes? By introducing cleaning standard sheets and delegating the work.

There are four easy steps to get past the problems and get on with the work.

1. **Designate the job title.** This is the easiest task: Clean the bathroom! Wash the dishes! Take out the trash!

Begin creating a cleaning standard sheet by printing the title of each job in bold letters at the top of an 8½" x 11" sheet of cardstock. Use a heavier paper so it will last through many handlings. After you have completed filling out your cleaning standards sheets, laminate them for even more durability.

2. **Detail the job duties.** This is an important step because different people have different methods and cleaning standards. For instance, your teenager may think cleaning the bathroom includes putting down the toilet lid, straightening the towels, and shutting all the drawers and doors. But you may include on the list cleaning the mirrors, washing out the sink, wiping down the counters, scrubbing the tub, shaking the rug, sweeping the floor, emptying the wastebasket, and mopping the floor.

Create a "Clean the Bathroom" cleaning standard sheet by listing what the family mutually agrees upon will be the methods and standards for cleaning the bathroom. List the jobs in sequential order. (Remember, start at the top and work down, begin at the cleanest place in the room and work to the dirtiest, pick up before cleaning up.) Be as detailed as possible so there will be no misunderstandings down the line. After the complete job description is listed on the sheet, make sure everyone again agrees to the cleaning standards that have been set. Repeat this process and create cards for all the regular chores around the house and yard.

I would recommend that you and your spouse write up proposed standards before you meet with your children to discuss them. It is always easier to start from someplace and make changes than to start from nothing and try to come to an agreement.

3. **Delegate the jobs.** This, of course, may bring out the sheriff in your household personalities. But work through the parameters and

CLEAN THE BATHROOM!

- ☐ Put dirty clothes in laundry basket
- ☐ Straighten towels
- ☐ Shake rugs
- ☐ Close vanity, drawers, and doors
- ☐ Empty wastebasket
- ☐ Clean mirrors
- ☐ Wipe down counters, clean out sinks, and shine taps
- ☐ Scrub and rinse bathtub and taps
- ☐ Shine bathtub taps
- ☐ Sweep and wipe up floor
- ☐ Clean toilet tank top, lid and seat (outside and in), exterior, rim, bowl. Flush.
- ☐ Confirm there is toilet paper on roll
- ☐ Return rugs to bathroom
- ☐ Look around once more and make sure it looks REALLY CLEAN AND INVITING!

assignments that will best meet the circumstances in your home. Make sure everyone who lives in the home is responsible for something on a frequent basis (depending on other obligations and time pressures), that everyone understands how long they will be doing their assigned jobs, and then review one last time the job titles, the details of the job duties, and the assignments.

While this may seem tedious and repetitive, it is easier to maintain the cleaning standards when all misunderstandings, confusion, and uncertainties have been addressed early on. It saves many exclamations of "But I didn't know!" and "No one told me!"

Of course there will be a training period where you will need to carefully, slowly, and patiently teach your children how to do a particular job. It takes repetition before they will be able to do a job easily and well. Help children stay at it until they have completed their chores correctly. This may mean helping them initially or setting a timer to keep them focused, but mostly encouraging, complimenting, and correcting them with grace. Just because they whine doesn't mean they shouldn't have to work until they can do their chores correctly.

4. **Delight in motivation.** Spouses, children, and teenagers enjoy doing housework more when there is motivation to keep it fun, a reason to work for a reward, and the anticipation of an activity afterward. The importance of incentives cannot be overstated, so seek for ways to implement a reward system that will work well in your home.

Use sticker charts for youngsters (to keep them interested), offer "after you are done" rewards for older children (which seems to work well for those children who love to play with friends, watch a video, or read a book), or promise a treat for the whole family (a trip to the park when the Saturday housework is done, a barbecue for those who have done their jobs for one week, an ice cream treat at dinnertime for those who have been cooperative and have not complained for one whole day). Whatever works for your family, seek to make work more like a game—and a fun one at that!

By using cleaning standard sheets to delegate housework responsibilities, you will keep the sheriff happy, you will help the slacker have definite reasons to work, you will clarify acceptable cleaning methods for the scrimper, and you will keep the complainer at bay. (He or she probably won't stop whining completely, but it will minimize the challenges as others begin to receive rewards and praise.)

So, the next time you run errands, buy a set of cardstock sheets at your nearest copy center, put your family's cleaning standards down in writing, and promote a standard of excellence in your home. It will make all the difference!

20

Teaching Your Family to Finish

I have seen the inner, private lives of many people. They are wonderful, usually hardworking, and interested in finding answers to their organizational needs.

But I also see a recurring challenge, a bad habit that many of us have. We "purchase, use, and push," meaning we push aside things we're finished with, instead of putting them where they need to go. In the really bad cases, our debris, treasures, and junk slowly moves outward from our walls, encroaching on our home and our lives. We purchase food and sundries (or sometimes even a larger, more expensive item like a television), and unpack the items and begin to use them. We discard and push to the side the plastic bags our purchases come in, the boxes and packing the TV is shipped in, and sometimes even the leftovers and fast-food restaurant containers.

All too soon the "purchase, use, and push" principle is practiced by the family in general. When children arrive home from soccer practice they grab a treat and, pushing their gear aside, eat their candy bar. The empty wrapper, sweaty clothes, and even the bag of soccer equipment often stays put until the next trip to the playing field.

When parents come home from work or school, they have their arms full of items from their errands that they put down on a convenient surface. Often the purchases are pulled from the shopping bags and unwrapped, but the shopping bags, wrapping, and sometimes even the items themselves are never really put away completely.

Is this habit present somewhere in your life? Is your master bedroom undone? Does your bathroom look a bit like a cyclone blew through? Or maybe your kitchen looks half like the stockroom of the grocery store and half like a recent tornado?

Wherever and however you might be afflicted by the "purchase, use, and push" pattern, there is a simple solution: finish.

Finish putting candy wrappers in the trash when you are done with your treat. Finish putting the groceries and shopping bags away when they are brought in the house. Finish throwing away the packaging when a large item is purchased, the newspaper is read, or a soda pop enjoyed.

The family that finishes—completely—whatever they are doing is the family that lives in an orderly house. So stop purchasing, using, and *pushing* and start purchasing, using, and *finishing*. It is a habit well worth cultivating and a way to develop better lifetime habits for those growing up in your home.

21

Do Something to Solve the Problem

M y mother was upset about it, but she never did anything about it."
I heard these words from a good friend the other day. You see,
some misbehavior this friend exhibited as a teenager was repeating itself in her own daughter and now she was stuck with a problem she didn't know how to solve. My friend had no precedent to cope with the problem, nor the necessary skills to correct it. She was upset about it, but didn't know what to do about it.

Bringing order into your life is more than neatly folding washcloths in the drawer, it is more than having the family room cleaned, and it is much, much more than having dinner on the table on time every night. It is about solving, resolving, and managing relationships and stewardships. This principle is so important and has such long-lasting consequences, I would encourage you to identify something in your life where you are now only "getting upset" and do something to solve the problem.

Do you have a four-year-old son who stoutly refuses to do his chores but is so cute in his stubbornness you hate to coerce him? Or a daughter who fails to do her weekly housework to an appropriate standard and yet wants to spend Friday evening with her friends? Or a spouse who could speak more softly and kindly to you about a recent cooking mistake you made?

You cannot change everything right away, but you can change something. Stand firm in your kindness, but be firm nevertheless. "Yes, I know you don't like to work, but your chores still need doing right away." "No, the bathroom is not clean enough. The rug still needs to be shaken. Then you may leave to be with your friends." "No, that tone of voice is not appropriate when speaking to me."

Say, "No." Say, "Not now." And then say, "Yes, I know I am a mean mom"—or a mean wife or aunt or grandma—"but enough is enough. This cannot continue."

This will make for a good beginning and can make all the difference in the long-term. You will not be popular just yet, but you will have done something beyond just getting upset about the problem. You will have *acted*.

I know I have some things to change about myself. I know I have things that I must "do something" about. So do you. So take a few minutes to write down a problem that needs addressing, list three or four ways to solve the problem, and then commit to do something about it. In the end, your effort to solve the problem will matter.

Being strong in the stewardships and relationships of your life, standing for what you feel is right, and remaining steady in your stance, will always bring more order to your life.

22

Health Care at Home

We usually don't think much about being organized for sickness until someone in the family gets a bad cold, a tender earache, or a case of the flu. Then we think about it plenty. It's no fun to wake up with a sore throat and find you have no lozenges to suck, or to get aches in your joints and discover you're out of pain medication, or to need something for a sour stomach and all you can find is a cracker.

Here are three simple ideas that will help you be ready for some of the most common sicknesses: buy a few "sickness" supplies, have a collection of over-the-counter medications, and set aside some special food for that tender tummy. Each of these can be considered a different project for a different day.

1. **Sickness medication.** Depending upon your own experience, you might want to purchase some throat lozenges, cough syrup, ear drops, some decongestant/antihistamine medications, and a variety of pain relief medicines. Get an ample supply to suit the needs of your family. Then when the earache starts in the middle of the night (which often seems to be the case with young children), you may be able to hold off going to the doctor until morning because of your close-at-hand numbing remedy. When the aches and pains set in, you will have medicine to relieve the

misery. When your children trouble you with their coughs, you can gently encourage a bit of medication to send them back to sleep. When your head gets stuffy, you can go to the bathroom cupboard to feel better instead of using up your energy in making a trip to the store.

2. **Sickness supplies.** For colds, flu, and allergies, you can purchase a good supply of tissues. It's convenient and more hygienic for the sick person to have his own box of tissues for his bedside. You can also provide a roll of personal toilet paper in the bathroom to confine the illness as much as possible.

To be prepared for upset stomachs, you can purchase a supply of gallon plastic bags. When someone gets sick, drape the edges of the bag over the edges of a medium-sized bowl and keep it handy. When the sickness erupts, they can simply upchuck into the bag, and then you can close and dispose. It is so much easier (for everyone) than the mad dash to the toilet that sometimes works and sometimes doesn't! It's also easier than cleaning up a kitchen bowl after each recurrence. This will work even for small children. Instead of making them run to the bathroom, they can just sit up, reach for the upchuck bowl, and let it go.

And don't forget some of the old standards: bandages, some kind of disinfectant, a thermometer, and perhaps a heating pad and a humidifier.

3. **Sickness food.** Some things just taste better when you are sick. These include cold lemon-lime soda (specifically 7-Up or Sprite), soft-set Jell-O (particularly raspberry and sometimes orange flavors), and instant butterscotch pudding (and occasionally vanilla). Some chicken noodle soup (along with oyster crackers) can really hit the spot whether you're suffering from a cold or stomach sickness. And when you finally feel like having a little bit to eat after a couple of days of emptying your stomach, yogurt and applesauce might be just what you need.

What helps your family when they are down and out? Stock up on these supplies and set them aside for those inevitable sick days ahead.

I hope you don't get ill any time soon, but if you or a member of your family does, the family nurse will be ready with some "sick" supplies to ease the runny nose, make the upchucks a bit easier, and have some yummy treats to calm down the queasy stomach.

23

Photograph Album Phobia?

Things are changing fast in the photography world, but many families still have plenty of photographic prints that need to be organized. For those with this need, several basic steps will get you in shape.

Before you start, though, realize that it takes a lot of time to get photos labeled and in a semblance of order, and even more time to get them in the appropriate photograph albums. Attempting this sort of a project in one, two, or even three sittings is just not possible. Instead, take this massive project (which you have probably been putting off for some time) and divide it into several thirty-minute sessions. (After it's all done, you just might want to try your hand at scrapbooking with some of the best photos. But that is a project for a later time and place.)

Here, then, are the steps to organizing photos:

1. **Gather your photographs together.** If you are like many people, your photos are scattered in several drawers, plastic containers, or boxes. No matter where your stash is located, start by gathering your photographs together.

2. **Label the back of each photo.** I like to use a fine-point, archival, felt-tip marker. Include at least three kinds of information in each label: The names of the people in the photo, the location of the photo (plus the

occasion, if appropriate), and the date. Be systematic and consistent in how you identify the position of the people in the photograph. For instance, you might list them as they are positioned from left to right, front to back. You can also use simple abbreviations in your caption: front row left to right can be indicated with "(front, l to r)," and so forth.

You'll proceed through the project faster if you set aside consistent times to label the photos. Perhaps you can leave them near your phone and label them during your casual phone conversations—it's a great multi-tasking project. Do a few at a time, but keep doing it. Labeled photos are essential for long-term sharing. (In the future, resolve to be disciplined and label your pictures as soon as they are developed or printed.)

As you are sorting through your photographs don't hesitate to discard photos that are embarrassing, inappropriate, or ugly. Do you really want others to know you looked like *that* during the overnight camping trip when it rained?

3. **Decide what general categories your photos should be organized into.** The categories you choose will flow naturally into the albums you end up with. Albums not only help organize your photos, but albums also provide a way of displaying and enjoying the photos. Some questions you'll want to consider are these:

- If you are married, will you have one album each for you and your spouse for those years before you met and married?
- Will you have a photo album of your family depicting your marriage, the arrival of the children, and family activities?
- Will you have an album for each of your children?
- Will you create a separate photo album for each of your major trips?
- Will you make a photo album of your grandchildren?
- Will you have an album for each family wedding or just one large one for all the marriages?
- Would you like to have an album of particularly artistic photos?
- Instead of topical albums, would you prefer a series of roughly chronological albums, which take you from the earliest photo taken to the most recent?

In addition to separate topical or chronological albums, will you have additional photo albums to organize all the photos you have ever taken? Or will you store those photos, by category, in separate boxes?

4. **Create category holders.** Once you have an idea of the categories you want to organize your photos into, create a separate holder for each category. You could tape together the sides of regular file folders and label the folder with the category name. Or purchase small plastic containers (perhaps 4" x 6" index-card holders, which will hold the most common sizes of photos) and label them. You will want one folder or container for each category you've identified. (If the container or folder becomes too full as you proceed with the sorting process, label a second one and add a "2" to the label. For example, the first folder can be called "Wedding Photos" and the second folder can be called "Wedding Photos—2.") These containers will act as tools for sorting.

5. **Sort the photographs.** Begin sorting through the labeled photos, putting them into the category containers. Photos of a single individual will likely go in that person's personal photo album, and thus would go into the corresponding folder or container (unless you're following a chronological method). Photos of family groups will likely go in the family photo album. Pictures of relatives might even go into an extended family photo album (if you ever get to that project). At this point, don't worry about sorting the photos within each folder. That will come later.

How do you deal with duplicate photos? After you have put the first copy of each photo in its appropriate folder, put the duplicates in additional sorting folders that you have labeled (from the perspective of your children) "My Brothers and Sisters," "My Parents," "My Grandparents," "My Cousins," and "My Friends." Then, as you set up the individual photo albums for your children, you can retrieve photos from these folders for filling out their photo albums. Not everyone's photo album will have the same pictures, but if you divide carefully, almost everyone's photo album will have a representation of these important people.

6. **Stack photos within the folders.** Take each folder and sort through the photos, stacking them by year. When that is done, take each year's stack and sort the pictures by month. Put each completed stack in

a smaller envelope, with the year written on the front. Return the labeled envelopes in order in the folder.

7. **Decide on the number of albums.** Now that your photos are in their category folders and are organized by year, decide how many albums you are going to set up, purchase that number, and label them. There are many types of photo albums to choose from. As you prepare to purchase yours, remember that photo albums need to last a long time, will be opened and viewed many times, and will likely take some abuse. Make sure you purchase albums of archival quality. More than one family's photographs have been ruined by putting them in an easy-to-mount, pre-glued photo album. Over time the glue seeps through the photos and ruins them. In other cases, inexpensive paper in photograph albums has literally fallen apart with age. So purchase with wisdom and care!

I personally prefer sturdy, archival photograph albums that allow flexibility for taking the pages out, moving the pages around, and adding pages when new photographs are found.

8. **Insert your photographs into the albums.** You are finally ready to put the photos in the photo albums. If possible, leave an extra space here or there to add photos as needed. It always seems another photo or two is found after the album is completed. Some experienced photograph album organizers suggest putting photographs only on the front side of the page to allow for expansion on the back side of each page as more photographs are collected and/or discovered.

As you do this, don't forget the folders you labeled "My Brothers and Sisters," "My Parents," "My Grandparents," "My Cousins," and "My Friends." You'll want to include some photos from these folders in various albums.

As you can see, preparing photographs for placement in albums is a long, albeit important project. If you have done nothing but collect photo prints, start now to make some sense of the mess. Keep working through your collection of photos, sorting, labeling, categorizing, and mounting as your spare time allows. Eventually you will have a nice collection of photo albums to share with family and friends and an easy system in place to organize the new photos you take and print.

24

Preparing for the Next Reunion This Reunion

I attended a family reunion recently. It was a gathering of extended family from all over the United States and Canada, all descendants of my husband's maternal grandparents. I learned several important things from this experience that might help when you next have a family reunion.

1. **Seize the moment.** Have an extra copy of the current contact list that every participant can check for accuracy as to names, home addresses, phone numbers, and e-mail addresses. And have some extra sheets so new friends and family can also record this important information. Doing this will make it easier for you to keep in contact—and will greatly facilitate preparing the list for the next reunion (with the few exceptions of people who move) in the meantime.

Part of seizing the moment is to always, always, always take pictures while you can. Some of those people probably won't make the next reunion, and those moments together are precious. Also, make notes about people you particularly connected with during your visit. For myself, I much enjoyed meeting extended family I had never seen before, including a judge who is also a mother of three, a former elementary school teacher who is now a stay-at-home mom, and a woman who is contemplating the responsibility of having her mother-in-law live in her home. We were kindred spirits of sorts, and it will be nice to contact them again soon. Taking notes that enable you to network with extended family members can bring great benefits down the line when you face the same problems as they are having now or have children who are going through similar challenges.

2. **Prepare for the next time now.** Consider making up a file titled "Our Next Family Reunion." Keep several things in it:

- An outline of this year's reunion. Include the schedule and notes about the specific places where you gathered, the games you played, the songs you sang, and the elements included in the program. Such annual notes will save a lot of time when it is your turn to host a reunion because the details (which so often fade from our memory) will be in print. Instead of wondering, you will just turn to your file and have this important information in front of you.
- Brief written notes giving your opinions about what happened and how you might do it differently next time: "The DVD slide show was great because they added music"; "The lunch was delicious except for the one purple salad"; "The name tags were prepared in triplicate and distributed all three mornings of the reunion to help people get to know each other better."
- Information about the professionals who smoothed the way: the business that made up the T-shirts, the printer who compiled the attractive address book, and the company that prepared the DVD slide show.

3. **Tie up the loose ends.** For instance, make sure you know how long everyone is staying so you can say good-bye. In our case, some of the relatives left one evening when I thought I'd see them the next day, and I didn't get to say my "love yous" and "I sure enjoyed our time together" and "hope we will see each other again soon." The next morning they were just gone, and I was left feeling empty and sad.

Also, when you say your own good-byes, make sure you say thank you to those who made it happen. And ask them what they learned and what they might do differently next time. Their observations will be invaluable.

Perhaps you are wondering why you need to prepare for the next family reunion even while you enjoy this one. After all, your turn might be several years away. But the truth is, those years will pass quickly. So seize the moment, keep good notes, take plenty of pictures, and tie up all the loose ends. These reunions don't happen often enough, and it's so easy to make preparations now that will save time, trouble, and hassle the next time around.

25

Streamlining the School
Time Schedule

Many mothers spend a good part of each year in the "school schedule." Their routine in sending their children off to school may or
may not be working well. Here are some ways to streamline the
"school schedule" routine to make the school year go easier with fewer
bumps. Ask yourself three questions to help identify problems. Each
question can lead to a separate project in organizing your home.

1. **Do I have a specific place where each child puts items that
need to be taken to school the next day?**

Consider obtaining a container that can serve as a confined place
where your child can put her backpack, school lunch money, apple for
tomorrow's science class assignment, and anything else she needs to take
to school. I like to have labeled plastic containers, one per child, for this
purpose. No one thinks completely clearly when they are in the rush to
get off to school. Gathering things the night before and putting it all in
one confined place makes good sense. It also allows your children to leave
each morning with confidence and ease.

2. **Do I have a specific routine for getting the children ready
for school each morning?**

For instance, children could be encouraged to decide the night before what they will wear to school. Their clothes should be laid out, complete with socks and shoes. Then tomorrow's dressing will be quick, decision-less, and easy. Try it—it makes all the difference!

Today's homework can be returned to their backpacks when it is completed. Signed permission slips can also be added, as well as the special book your child is reading out loud in class.

3. **Do I have a breakfast clean-up routine my children can participate in?**

I know many families have cold cereal on school mornings, but you can still have an established routine for getting the table set and each child's dishes cleared after they've eaten. Add to that a routine that includes getting their teeth brushed (and the toothpaste lid put back on and the toothbrush put away). These routines can include a set time for beginning breakfast, assignments for who will do what in terms of setting out the food and dishes and putting it all away, a time for brushing teeth, and so forth. Consider posting the information on a fun chart that you hang in a prominent place in the kitchen.

I suggest that this week you slow down and focus on working with each child individually until he or she has learned these simple habits. Each new habit will make for long-term benefits—and your child will be off to school feeling less rushed, less stressed, and better prepared to face the day.

26

Getting Homework Done

One of the many concerns of parents (and sometimes grandparents and other caretakers) is getting a child's homework done in a timely manner. As you get your children ready for the school year, a deep worry can settle into your soul. How will they do this year? What at school or home will have the greatest impact on them? Is there anything more I can do to help them?

My own experience has shown me the answer to the last question is a resounding "Yes!" Here are three ways you can make a difference.

1. **Set up a routine place,** quiet and secluded (but within your everwatchful supervision), where your children can do their homework.

I know some families have a quiet hour after school when the kitchen table is the "homework table," with rules that include no talking, no facemaking, and no silly noises. In other words, there is a serious attempt to keep them focused on their work.

When the homework is ready to be checked, the mother or another adult quietly talks to the child in the same room, but in a far corner, about what has been done right and wrong. After making the necessary corrections, the child is free to leave the "homework table" and pursue other, more fun, activities.

I know other mothers who have found that a personal desk in the child's bedroom is very helpful for homework, especially as their children have matured and become more independent. With a small overhead bookshelf, personal office supplies, and a good light, the child finds homework time also a time to be alone, to think, to wonder, and to dream (which sometimes isn't exactly the idea). Generally, if the child is left in his or her room until the homework is finished and can't do anything else until it is finished correctly, he or she will get to the task soon enough.

2. **Have a regular time each day for homework.** I know some mothers who let their children play with friends for an hour or so after school lets out; then the family gathers back home for homework. They feel that this tends to get out the wiggles, refreshes their minds, and makes them more likely to be willing to turn to the task.

Other mothers find it is better to feed their children a snack, pull out the books, and get the homework finished before friends are allowed into the house or the children are allowed to go out and play.

Of course, there will be some days when the schedule is totally changed because of extracurricular activities such as piano lessons, dance team, or football. But even on those days there needs to be time set aside for getting the homework done.

3. **Motivate with rewards.** Children often find it hard to stick to the homework task if they don't have motivation to keep them going. Try reminding them of something wonderful, exciting, or interesting that will follow. "We will watch a short video when you are finished!" "I will serve an extra piece of cake to everyone who gets their homework finished and checked before Dad gets home!" "You may have John over to play when your homework is finished!"

With these patterns of "Let's get the homework finished!" set in a child's routine, the child usually give less and less resistance to doing it, especially if the parents remain firm yet kind in insisting that homework is both important and a priority.

Some children need more supervision and encouragement than others. I know one mother whose daughter struggled with reading long past the normal time for children to "get it." However, the mother patiently worked each day with the child, helping her and motivating her with attention and encouragement. It took longer for this girl to get her homework finished than was the case with most of her siblings, but once she understood reading, she turned out to be the best and fastest one of them all. She soon hit her stride, and off she went to become more independent, self-motivating, and creative than her mother could have ever expected.

So set aside a time and a place, get creative with motivators, and be patient with the "slower" one. Homework routines will soon become a natural part of your children's days, and they will understand you mean business when you say it is homework time. And they will be better students for your diligence.

Good luck during the school year! I know, because I have been there, that every day you help your children get through their homework is one day closer to them turning out to be mature, delightful, creative adults—who will thank you frequently for being firm about homework during this critical time of their lives!

27

Saving Children's Paperwork Treasures

Many families have an overabundance of treasured children's paperwork. There are homework papers, art work, certificates, and programs. What should be kept and what should be discarded? How much is enough? How do you organize the things you keep? Where and how should it be stored?

You need only so many original drawings from a particular season of the child's life to represent his or her artistic interests for that period, so select carefully what you save. Children will bring home far more school paperwork than you will want to keep, so mainly keep items that are particularly creative or highly amusing. It is sometimes wise to set homework papers aside in a "To File" folder for a month or so before deciding which of the many papers brought home will be kept. This allows some seasoning to take place before final decisions are made.

Also, children don't want to remember anything but the best of their schoolwork, so save only their 100 percent spelling tests; near-perfect science, math, and history tests; and papers with positive teacher comments. At the same time, be sure to save everything autobiographical the child writes! These will become priceless as time passes.

School projects that are too large for keeping in the binder might best be displayed in the home for a month or so. Then, as the season for display wanes, take a picture of the child with the project. The photos can be saved without the hassle and volume of large science projects, drama scenery, and three-dimensional crafts gathering dust in the home. (This suggestion excludes any and all items that might be reused for younger siblings' needs. Many a science project has seen an appropriate reuse to save the parents time and trouble.)

Once you've decided what to keep, you need to have a good way to organize it. I suggest a simple, systemized approach. This approach will lead you to an ongoing series of organizing projects as you put the plan into action.

Begin by purchasing the following, available at most office-supply stores:

- An 8½" x 11" sturdy "view" binder for each child in your family (A different color for each child makes it easy to find the right binder on the shelf—this means Jake will have green binders, Gloria will have blue, and Marianne will have red.)
- 20 binder dividers for each child
- A 250-sheet ream of 67-pound 8½" x 11" archival cardstock
- A good supply of plastic sheet protectors
- A supply of archival glue sticks
- Some self-sticking photo corners
- A three-ring plastic pencil holder
- A three-hole paper punch

Once you've made your purchases, you can begin your initial setup. Prepare a simple cardstock cover sheet to slip into the "view" front and back of the binder, plus another for the spine to further identify the binder's owner. Take the twenty binder dividers you purchased for each child and label them with all the years from his or her birth until he or she will be twenty (at which time we hope they will be taking care of their own journaling needs). Three-hole punch a stack of the cardstock and put it in the rear of each binder, along with plenty of plastic sheet protectors. Put the three-ring plastic pencil holder in the front of the binder; this is where you can keep the glue sticks, photo corners, and writing pens handy for updating the journals. Now you are ready!

When you decide a piece of children's paperwork is worth keeping, three-hole punch it and put it in the binder behind the appropriate year's divider. If the paper is too small to punch and put in the binder (a newspaper announcement of the birth of your child, for example), glue it to a piece of cardstock, write any comments you desire, and place the cardstock sheet in the child's binder behind the appropriate divider. You can add other small items to this same sheet of cardstock as you find them. Some items, like certificates, might better be saved by inserting them in the sheet protectors. Other items might be suitable for mounting using the photo corners and attaching them to the cardstock sheets that are then put in the sheet protectors.

If you don't have a lot of time right when a piece of paper needs storing, slip it into a plastic sheet protector and put it behind the appropriate year's divider. This will keep it safely stored until you have extra minutes to properly mount it.

As each child's binder becomes filled with paperwork treasures, you can purchase and label another binder of the same color (Jake's #2 Journal Binder). Put the unused labeled dividers and supplies into this new binder, and you are ready for more paperwork. For most children, about six to ten binders will be enough to hold all their important "paper" journal items until they are finished with high school and beginning their further education.

Family members will immensely enjoy going through their journals as they grow up, looking at their more rudimentary artwork, their simplistic handwriting, and their attempts at written communication.

As a side note, each child can also have a sturdy storage box for his or her bulkier treasures, one box per child. Encourage them to personalize their treasure box with drawings, stickers, or other artwork and then use it to keep their bulkier valuables. This helps confine messes that would otherwise spill out into their bedrooms and sometimes other areas of the house.

Now that you have things organized, it takes only minutes to find the right child's binder, punch paperwork, and put it behind the right divider. And once you have your system set up, you'll be able to enjoy your children's journals for many years to come.

28

Managing Children's Clothes

Storing unused children's clothing (i.e., those items that have grown too small or that are still too big or that are out of season) in an organized manner can be an unpleasant chore—unless you have a system set up that works well. If you do, then it is easy and convenient. So let's get going and get all those extra, unneeded clothes, socks, and shoes out of their bedrooms and safely put away for the next child, the next growth spurt, the next season, or the next of kin.

1. **Gather containers.** Purchase, find, or collect containers that will be useful for long-term storage. I prefer those that will fit on the shelves above the closet rod in the children's closets (although the containers will also spend some time in storage areas located elsewhere). They should be stackable (when empty or full), sturdy, and clean.

If you purchase plastic containers, choose those that have well-fitting lids and are semi-opaque to make it easier to see the contents. The semi-opaque quality of the container will also allow for easy labeling of the boxes, as described below. This storage container investment will be worthwhile because you will be able to use these containers over and over again until your children are grown.

How many containers do you need? I suggest having at least two boxes for each year of your children's ages (one for spring/summer clothes, another for fall/winter clothes). For example, if you have three children aged two, five, and eight, you will want two boxes for each age, two boxes for storing clothes that are either too big or too small, one for the spring/summer season, and one for fall/winter.

Sometimes when I suggest so many boxes, people just laugh at me and say they can't possibly devote that much space to storing clothes. If you are in that category, you can use one box for every year of age (eliminating the separation into summer and winter clothes) or even just one box for every two years of age. Using this method saves space, but it makes for a little more hassle when getting in and out of the boxes.

You might also consider gathering containers for shoes, socks, swimwear, winter accessories, costumes, and underwear. These kinds of items are easy to store together, and they seem to be needed frequently.

2. **Organize each child's clothing.** Sometimes it works best to do one child's clothing all at once. This may mean letting your children share an afternoon at a neighbor's house (and then returning the favor for your friend). It may mean neglecting your ringing phone and doorbell. With focus and hard work, you can empty your child's closet and chest of drawers one item at a time and put into your containers the clothes you wish to store (strategically place the containers around the room for the greatest efficiency).

After sorting through the clothes, pick out outfits you want your children to use right now. If you have young children who are learning to get dressed themselves, try to have all the clothing match all the other clothing—otherwise, creative youngsters can come up with some mighty interesting combinations. (Yes, you will also want to have a dress-up box handy for those creative moments.)

I also suggest leaving out one set of nice dress clothes for Sundays or special occasions for the boys and two sets for the girls (this seems to work until they're teenagers, when they'll want more variety—but by then they'll be choosing themselves what to keep in the closet and what to store).

You can keep more clothes out if you need or want to, but, for the most part, I recommend you keep most of your children's unneeded clothing stored away. Young children don't need a lot of clothes to be happy. They simply have their minds on a lot of other things, so keep it simple.

In addition to the seasonal boxes, you can have boxes for specialty items, as mentioned above—shoes, socks, underwear, and so forth. You can put similar items in large, clear zip-top plastic bags and label them accordingly: "1-year-old boy's socks," "2-year-old girl's socks," and so forth. Then put the bags inside the "socks" box. Not only does this help you be more organized, but it also allows you to buy socks on sale and have a place to keep them until they are needed. The same method can be used for underwear or other small items of clothing.

3. **Label the containers.** You can label a container by printing its primary contents on two sheets of cardstock. Use large letters so you won't have to squint to see them. Then put a label just inside opaque plastic the container or on the outside of a cardboard box, on each end.

For example, if you have three children aged two, five, and eight, you could have two boxes labeled "1-year-old summer" and "1-year-old winter" (for those clothes that have recently been outgrown), two boxes labeled "2-year-old summer" and "2-year-old winter," and two boxes each for all the other years to eight years old. You may also need two boxes labeled "9-year-old summer" and "9-year-old winter" for the clothes that are just a bit too big for the oldest child. If you have boys and girls, you can also divide the clothes accordingly, with "1-year-old girl's summer" and "1-year-old boy's summer" clothes containers.

4. **Put the extras in storage.** After you have filled and labeled your containers, store them where they will be convenient and yet out of the way (usually in the basement, garage, or attic). When you find a child is rapidly growing out of the clothes they are currently wearing, go to your storage containers, store the undersized items, and pull out new, larger clothing. Of course, this will need to be done whether or not there is a change of the seasons. (It's funny how children seem to grow the most between the time when you buy them pants for the new school year and when school actually starts.)

5. **An "Items to Be Stored" container.** To keep up on your new

system, it may be helpful to keep one open storage container labeled "Items to Be Stored." Then when life becomes rushed and you have children's clothing that needs to be sorted and stored, you'll have a temporary landing place for these items. It helps keep all such clothes confined and conquered!

This week you can set up a children's clothing storage system. It will make everything easier at your house, from cleaning up their rooms to doing their laundry.

29

Organizing Children's Toys

Organizing toys, like most other home organization projects, can best be simplified and managed by identifying three different types of children's toys in your home.

1. **Large toys.** These are furniture-type, bulky toys, not easily confined in a box or in a cupboard, and tend to look messy whenever they are out because children rarely leave anything neat, squared off, or upright. These large toys might also include bikes, plastic play houses, rocking horses, or anything else, indoors or outdoors, that is bulky and cumbersome. These items are best stored by designating a specific "home" for them where they can be stored as the house or yard is cleaned up. One way to help teach your children where these items belong is to hang simple signs on the walls for the indoor toys and tape or paint lines on the garage floor for the outdoor toys and bikes.

2. **Medium-sized toys.** Children seem to always enjoy having a lot of their toys out at once, which means there always seems to be a mess. To help contain the clutter I suggest sending most of these medium-sized toys "on vacation." Label large plastic containers with the names of various vacation spots. The bins at our house, for example, are labeled

Philadelphia, Cincinnati, Chicago, San Francisco, Baltimore, Columbus, and Atlanta. You could also use more exotic or even imaginary places.

Divide the toys into the containers. The children are allowed to choose one box of toys at a time. When they are finished playing with the toys from "Chicago," they put them away, and then may choose another box of toys. Remember, the smaller the mess, the more ready and willing children will be to clean up.

3. **Tiny toys.** These are the bits and pieces of larger toys and include Legos, doll clothes and accessories, Lincoln Logs, and puzzles. These tiny toys are best confined to zip-top clear plastic bags, which are then labeled for ease of identification and storage.

Some tiny toys—like Legos—have so many tiny pieces that storing them in a single bag is not practical. In those cases, I suggest designating an entire large container for them. When the children want to play with the toy, spread a sheet on the floor and place the toys in the center. When the children are finished playing with the toys, simply gather up each corner of the sheet and deposit the entire thing it into its labeled container. As long as the children have kept the pieces confined to the sheet, drawing up of the corners automatically cleans up the entire area. With the area clean, the children may again choose another box of toys.

I use standardized boxes, wall bookshelves, and clear plastic containers for my children's toys so I can line them up along the children's bedroom wall and keep them out of the way. The house is never very messy with children's toys because it is never allowed to get that way.

I hope these ideas help you control and contain your children's toys. There are many good library books to peruse or home improvement store books that have creative and innovative ideas to decoratively store childhood toys. Whether they are large, medium, or small, children's toys can be organized and your life simplified. Remember: divide, confine, and conquer!

ORGANIZE
YOUR TIME

30

Gaining "Time Alone" to Focus

I suffer from DRD or Delayed Response Disorder. I know there are many different significant and challenging disorders that are serious and require medical attention, counseling, and much training to deal with and overcome, but my disorder comes with just being alive. We have been taught that we are supposed to be *here,* ready and willing to respond to our loved ones gently, kindly, and without hesitation. But when I focus, I am *gone.* When someone—anyone—comes up to me and asks me a question or makes a comment or even submits a demand, it takes me a second to come back to the here and now, switch mental gears, and be able to respond.

While some of you may suffer from this particular challenge, I suspect that if you are a busy mom with lots of kids or a father with a crowd of teenagers or an entrepreneur juggling a family and a home business, there are probably days when you are so busy and overwhelmed that you may need a moment to switch mental gears and be able to respond to the request at hand.

We all need some alone time. We need some silence. We need some space to think through our priorities and our relationships and to let our minds rest. So what do we do when our busy-ness of life interferes with the business of life?

May I suggest three different ways that have helped me have a calmer, more peaceful home life?

1. **Train your children to let you have some time alone** for twenty-minute increments several times a day. This training can begin as soon as your children are old enough to want their own "time alone." After explaining the concept of "time alone," begin by separating from your family for five minutes, then ten minutes, then fifteen minutes, and finally twenty minutes.

Often you may still be in the same room as your children, available to offer comfort or maintain a watchful eye, but it is good for your children to learn how to respect your need for space, silence, and some "time alone." In turn, make sure you let them have their own time alone when you will not interrupt them and ask them to do chores, set the table, or put away laundry. When you give your children their space, they will also be more willing to respect the space you require from time to time.

So set a timer and set some rules: no questions, no interruptions, and no comments until the timer dings.

2. **Take regular walks.** A good, long walk each day to the park, or around the block, or even just down to the stop sign and back is one of the best ways to get away from the phone, from the television, from the radio, and from interruptions. Sometimes you have to physically be gone in order to find the opportunity to be mentally and emotionally gone, too. Taking walks may allow you the time alone you need to make sense of your particular circumstances, your challenges, and your emotions.

3. **Ask an older child to be responsible for the younger children** while you spend a few minutes alone working on a project in your bedroom or the home office. Shut the door, ignore the phone, and focus.

When you make some time each day to be *gone,* you will find it easier to be *here,* available and ready to answer questions, settle disputes, and tackle the challenges of your day.

31

Outside-In or Inside-Out?

Are you an outside-in or an inside-out person? For myself, it seems that I swing between the two personalities. Sometimes I try to avoid, delay, or otherwise let my "inside" private routines languish in hopes that things will hold together while I focus on my "outside" life. But my hair gets dirtier and dirtier, my nails begin to fray and break, my head begins to hurt because I have not eaten regularly nor slept soundly, and then I know I am in trouble.

So I revert to "inside-out." I take an overly long time to get my routines back in order again. I wash my hair, I trim my nails, I focus on eating when the clock strikes the right hour, and I try to go to bed at a decent time. But just when I get my personal routine settled down again, back I go to trying to beat the clock, to do without my regular personal routine, hoping that things will hold together again for just an extra day or two. Finding time to be orderly in your personal habits is a great foundation for all other organization projects you might attempt.

Once I understood this pattern in my personal habits, I worked on becoming a regular tick-tock person. I do what needs to be done for me to keep my inside clock ticking nicely and routinely as I get up and get ready each day (on the difficult days, this is sometimes the bare minimum).

Then I spend a few minutes on my inside routine again at night before retiring. It has to be *me* first and then *them*. I can't let my "inside" needs go unattended for very long, just as I can't ignore my "outside" needs altogether. Instead, I need to pace myself: go slowly, be steady, and keep a good balance. In this way I can feel good about myself and still try to "save the world" on a regular basis.

In the same way, I have learned to eat my meals at regular times. Instead of being focused on a project and ignoring my rumbling stomach at lunchtime (which is the easiest meal for me to skip or delay), I watch the clock, and I eat some time between noon and one o'clock. This keeps my blood sugar up, my mind alert, and my body active without any more work or time on my part. It is a matter of finding time to take care of me.

Finally, I keep up with my personal clothing repairs, alterations, and mending. If a button comes off, it goes back on. If a hem comes down, the hem goes back up. These personal "inside" chores take only minutes, but if left undone, we look undone and our wearable wardrobe shrinks smaller and smaller. I do something every day that will maintain my "inside" routines and help my "outside" routine function at a well-organized level.

It must be tick-tock: your personal care first on a scheduled, regular basis each day, and then the "outside" work of caring for those you love and serve in your world. It always seems to work best that way.

32

Starting Your Morning the Night Before

I cannot overemphasize the importance of doing essential routine items when there isn't a lot of stress. This especially applies to sunrise routines. Early morning is usually not the best time to make decisions, prepare for the day, or finalize plans. Whenever possible, start your day the night before. The morning is for getting ready and getting out the door. So how can you have better, more organized mornings?

1. **Make decisions the night before.** Decide what you are going to wear tomorrow, tonight. Decide when you need to leave tomorrow to be at your destination on time, and work backward to know when you should set the alarm clock. Decide what you will serve for breakfast—and get the English muffins out of the freezer so you won't have to thaw them in the microwave before you can even begin to think about toasting them. Decide in what order you will tackle your morning tasks so if something doesn't get done and has to wait until later, you will have done the most essential jobs first.

2. **Prepare the night before.** What about setting the breakfast table right after the dinner dishes are finished? It is just as much work as setting in the morning, but it is half the hassle because you are not under so much stress. What about preparing your children's sack lunches in the

evening to facilitate a more unhurried morning routine? You might even pack up the car for the errands so tomorrow morning you only have to get yourself (and maybe your children) in the car.

3. **Finalize plans the night before.** Does everyone in the family know what is happening tomorrow? When will Dad be home? When and where will Mom pick up the children at school for piano lessons? What special tasks or chores need to be done before the children can play with their friends or watch a video? Children and adults alike don't like surprises, mistakes, or waiting. Try to avoid them as much as possible by discussing tomorrow's plans tonight at the dinner table. Make sure everyone in the family knows exactly what to expect, when to expect it, and what the backup plan is if things don't go as planned.

If things aren't going smoothly for you, try a simple change to "forward" routines and see how much it helps. Making decisions the night before, preparing for tomorrow the night before, and finalizing plans the night before will make a tremendous difference in the level of chaos, stress, and tension of your mornings.

33

Running Errands without Running Yourself Ragged

I run errands—a lot. I am sure you do, too! For me, there are three problems I struggle with: (1) I get somewhere and don't have what I need to finish my errands; (2) I get somewhere and wish I had a piece of information or an item to do another errand nearby; and (3) I complete my errands and am heading home when I remember I have forgotten one or more errands. So what can be done? Let's stop and work through some methods that will permanently solve these problems.

1. **Do it now.** Always put whatever you need to complete your errands in your vehicle as soon as you think about it. Need to take a shirt to the dry cleaners? Put it in the vehicle *now!* Need to return some books to the library? Put them in the vehicle *now!* Need to drop something off at a friend's house? Put it in the vehicle *now!* I keep a large plastic container in the back of my van to keep these items contained, organized, and easy to retrieve.

Then add these errands to your "errands list." I keep my list on a folded sheet of 8½" x 11" paper that I attach to a half-sized clipboard. This small-sized clipboard has become one of the best investments I have made because the clipboard keeps my errands list safe as I shuffle papers around on my desk. I know my list will be attached to something sturdy and can be easily found.

I finish preparing for my errands by walking around the house, garage, and yard to see if there is anything else I can accomplish while I am out running errands. This helps me take care of stray projects that might have missed my notice and reduces the number of times I have to be out each week.

2. **Make a list.** I keep several index cards in the outside pocket of my wallet so I have something handy where I can write down any items I need to buy as soon as I think of them. For instance, I have an index card for the hardware store, the variety store, and the nearby strip mall (dry cleaners, post office, and shoe repair). When I think of something I need to do or purchase, I make a note on the appropriate card. Then when I am shopping at the variety store and realize I am near the hardware store, I can pull out my "Hardware Store" index card list, see that I need to buy a can of putty, and can stop there without much fuss.

3. **Have a plan.** Never leave the house to do errands without a written list of the places you need to go, the errands to be done at each stop, and the sequence in which you will run your errands. I usually make up my list gradually as I think about it. If I don't write it down now, I won't remember it later. I leave room between each item on my list to add any details that I may think of later. If an errand on my list requires me to take an item with me, I circle that errand on the list which acts as a second reminder in case I have not yet put the item in the car. Then before I leave, I number my errands in the order in which I plan to do them.

I try to plan my errands in a logical progression as often as possible so that I rarely have to turn left across traffic and can more easily find parking places on the street in front of the establishments I visit.

Finally, I have learned to prepare to run my errands several hours before I actually leave, which means sometimes doing it the night before. I like to do my preparation early because I have found that the worst time for me to be planning is when I am getting ready to go. I am usually rushed, get a phone call, have several interruptions from family members, or am running late, which means I don't have time to stop, think, and do it right. So, if you're like me, you'll want to prepare for all your errands early.

Try these new errand techniques and see if things don't go a bit better for you!

34

Using Your Waiting Time Profitably

hate to wait. I don't like waiting at traffic lights, standing in checkout lines at the grocery store, or being delayed at the bank. Lengthy dentist's and doctor's office waits are beyond annoying. Even the wait during the last few minutes before your spouse walks in the door from work can be unbearable. How do you reduce wasted time and more profitably use your minutes when you're powerless to do anything but wait, wait, and wait some more?

First, look for ways to reduce the waiting time altogether. For instance, running your errands early in the day usually reduces the amount of time you have to wait in line. The bank, the post office, and the grocery store are often rather empty and you can breeze through the errands on your list with less time and trouble. You might even be able to do some of your errands by mail or over the Internet, such as ordering stamps or sending in a deposit to the bank.

Second, shop by phone as much as possible. Call ahead to see if the video you want to rent is available and can be held at the front desk. Call to see if the item you desire to buy is in stock at the local hardware store. Arrange for pickup and delivery by any company offering such a service without charge.

Third, whenever you make an appointment, say, at the doctor's or dentist's office or the beauty salon, ask for the first appointment in the morning or the first appointment in the afternoon. While this doesn't completely ensure your dentist or doctor will see you on time, it does improve your chances. Often you can make your life even easier by calling the office before you leave home to ask if they are on schedule. It is nicer to wait at home, finishing up a project here or there, than to be sitting in a waiting room.

If you have done all you can to avoid waiting and still find yourself "on hold," how can you use that time more effectively? Here are three different activities you might like to try.

1. **Carry reading materials with you at all times.** My favorites, of course, are paperbacks about home organization or booklets that share home management tips. I learn a great deal during those inevitable minutes waiting because I am prepared to open a book and read. I keep a red pen handy for noting those items I wish to implement into my own routines, tools I will consider buying, and different systems to improve my use of time. I keep a paperback in each of my vehicles and one in my purse. When I am going to be waiting with children, I carry "read aloud" books for them and use the time to share a story. Sometimes other children in the waiting room gather around us to hear the story as well. It seems like the waiting time always goes faster when a story is being told. Having your own books with you means you can use your waiting time to read alone or aloud, which can truly benefit you and your family's life.

2. **Bring along a small kit consisting of stationery or cards, pens, envelopes, and stamps.** So many thank-you notes, birthday wishes, and congratulations can be written during the long minutes waiting for a doctor's appointment. Sometimes I even have time to slip the note inside a greeting card, sign it, and send it off. One more item off my "to do" list. It seems to be a law of life that the waiting time seems to diminish in proportion to the amount of good use you can make of that waiting time, so prepare well!

3. **Begin a memorization program.** Even if you have intermittent waits in lines or in traffic, you may find there is still enough time to

memorize a short saying. Select four or five short sayings that you feel might benefit your life—maybe a quote from a good book, a poem, or an inspirational thought from a wise leader. One of my favorite recent quotations is "Good, better, best. Never rest 'til good be better and better best." Write the quotes on index cards and tuck them behind the visor in your vehicle or in your wallet. Begin committing the quotes to memory during your "wasted" time.

These quotations can benefit your life immediately and can also be shared with others (particularly unruly children when they need to be occupied). View your waiting time as a chance to learn something new or to teach something to someone else. Children and teenagers often enjoy the challenge of learning something new that someone they admire already knows.

There are countless other ways to be prepared to use your waiting time profitably. Do you knit or crochet? Can you teach one of your children that skill during those repetitive orthodontist visits? Do you have a regular waiting time with one child while another child is finishing up piano or dance lessons? Can you teach your child the alphabet or counting numbers (forward or backward) during your wait?

As you look at your schedule, identify your "waiting time" pockets. Try to reduce or eliminate them. Then prepare to use the time profitably by bringing along something to do yourself or to teach and share. You will soon find your life filled with more feelings of accomplishment and your frustrations considerably reduced.

35

Managing Monday Morning Madness

I have struggled for years with a malady I call "Monday Morning Madness." Maybe you do, too. It seems somehow that if Monday morning goes really well, the rest of the week goes just as well. Of course, every Monday morning you *know* you are going to finish *everything* important and essential this week as soon as possible. But if you have just one unavoidable repair, unexpected interruption, or unplanned activity right at the beginning of the week, your Monday (and sometimes your whole week) seems to fall apart.

So how do you conquer your Monday Morning Madness? Here are five skills that can relieve the stress, dampen the depression, and keep you going all week long.

1. **Make a list before Monday begins.** More than any other single stress-relieving technique, making a list of what's on your mind is essential to success. This task is usually best done on Sunday evening after you have had a chance to rest and before a new week begins. Your "to do" list will sometimes be long and frustratingly difficult. No matter—write down everything that is troubling you and needs your attention.

2. **Set priorities.** Weigh each item on your list according to importance and prioritize it using the A-B-C-D system. If it is *essential,* it gets an

"A" priority. If it is *important,* it gets a "B." If it would be *nice* to have done, it gets a "C." If it can *wait,* it gets a "D."

3. **Pace yourself.** Now with your prioritized list in hand, review the upcoming week and begin scheduling your "to do" items, beginning with your "A" priorities. Decide which day and time will be best to address each "A" item. When you are running errands on Tuesday, could you add two "A" errands to your list and make them a part of the trip? Can you read the "A" article on Wednesday while you are waiting during piano lessons? Can your spouse help with that "A" repair on Saturday morning (after you have had a good hot breakfast together)?

Add "B" items to each day's schedule as appropriate, remembering that "B" items are to be done *only if time allows.* List the "C" items at the bottom of your daily schedule to be tackled only if there is *plenty of extra time* or if someone kindly asks you if there is something they can do to help.

Remember, always do the most important things first!

4. **Leave time for the inevitable interruption.** It seems inevitable that just as you are ready to go, you'll discover your vehicle has a flat tire; just when you arrive at the specialty store, you'll find it closed; or just as you sit down for a moment's rest, you'll be needed by someone with an urgent emergency. Such challenges are distressing, but know that every day for the rest of your entire life there will be some challenge, some repair, or some problem to be solved. Plan on it. Allow time for it. That way your Monday mornings—and your whole week—won't be ruined by unexpected problems.

5. **Stop and rest.** You can work and work until you are past weariness, but that is not wise! Being overworked makes you cranky and sometimes means preparing a burnt dinner and often means an unhappy family. (Have you ever noticed that your family is just as happy as you are?) Listen to your body and stop and rest before you run out of energy. Even taking just a few minutes to rest, to regroup, and to get a grip can be helpful. And if you don't stop to rest, it takes that much more energy to finish your work and that much longer to renew yourself at the end of the day.

Remember, Monday mornings are going to come every week. So take time to plan, prioritize, pace yourself, and plan for the inevitable. Watch your energy level. Keep a smile on your face and that A-B-C-D list in your hand. Then go to work! With practice and patience, Monday Morning Madness will not overcome your capacity to remain serene and graceful as you contemplate each new week.

36

Schedule Reminders Early

S ometimes we get so focused on a big event in our lives—a wedding, a funeral, a business trip, a two-week visit from a relative—we forget other smaller, but not less important, celebrations for family and friends. Occasionally our forgetting results in some offense being taken, and then it becomes even harder to make it right. Have you had this experience before, too?

If so, there is a simple method to help us handle all the events—large *and* small—that we want to remember: schedule reminders early.

I once missed an important birthday because it was on the third day of the month, and by the time I remembered to turn the page on my calendar, it was too late to send a birthday card or make a phone call on the day of the celebration. I decided right then to make preparations to avoid another disaster. I pulled out my calendar and made a list of all the birthdays, anniversaries, or celebrations that fell within the first week of any month. Then I made a note about each celebration on the first day of the last week of the month prior to the event. In other words, in addition to noting the actual date of the event, I scheduled a reminder for myself several days in advance.

I did the same thing with a weeklong speaking engagement I had one summer. I made a note in the middle of July (when I am less stressed) to begin preparing for my August speaking commitment. Because I scheduled my reminders early, I had enough time to prepare my speaking notes, my visual aids, and my handouts *early*. I was even able to complete the last-minute details of the project before the deadline.

It is so helpful to begin early, to decide what you will do with each and every responsibility that comes your way. With an early beginning (usually started in the nicer, calmer days of your life) you can gain confidence and find better pacing, ensuring greater success. Don't wait to start until after it is too late to do it right!

There are so many times and places where we can look ahead and thus avoid disasters, embarrassing moments, and otherwise untimely incidents. For me, it helps to look ahead into next month (and maybe the next and the next) to see where I might be more timely and where I might be able to prepare for an upcoming deadline. Who knows, I might be sick, forget, or have a sudden emergency that prevents me from meeting my deadline or remembering a special celebration. But if I look ahead, make good written notes, and plan and prepare as needed, I am more likely to be calm, collected, and capable—no matter what!

So take a few minutes and look at your upcoming commitments, appointments, and special events. Ask yourself what you can do to avoid potential disasters. What can you do *now* to be ready for *then?* Add these preparation notes and projects to your calendar, and schedule time in your routine during the less-stressful times. That way, when the heat is on, you will be coolly floating above the meltdown. Happy scheduling!

37

Timers and Reminders

'm a forgetter, especially when life gets difficult, stressful, or I have too much to do in too little time. I forget to put new checks in the checkbook. I put bread in the oven and walk away and forget it's there, turning darker and darker with each minute. I have even boiled eggs until the water is all gone, the bottom of the pan is burnt, and the eggs are all but vaporized. Once in a while I will even leave my home not quite completely dressed. When these kinds of things happen, I remind myself of two things:

First, it is not shameful to be short on RAM—the place in your mind where your brain handles the small details of life. Maybe you are just wired differently than the person down the street who doesn't seem to ever have to write a note about anything and remembers everything perfectly.

Second, maybe you have a lot of RAM, but it is busy handling some stress in your life, dealing with a difficult problem at work, or figuring out how to get the laundry done this weekend between all the other competing pressures.

Whatever the reason you may have that causes you to tend to forget, adjust to it the best you can by finding easy ways to remember.

In order to keep myself safe, to function the best I can when I know the days are going to be long, and to continue living with people without constant embarrassment, I have discovered three solutions that work for me. Maybe they will work for you, too.

1. **I have self-initiated "timers and reminders"** to warn me long before I might embarrass myself by forgetting something important. For instance, when I am ready for an appointment, but have a few minutes before I have to leave, I set a timer to remind me when I should wrap up a last-minute project I might be working on and prepare to leave. The timer keeps me from becoming so distracted that I work past when I should be climbing into the car. Also, I keep a checkbook register in my wallet to record all my purchases, whether by check, debt card, or cash. This method keeps me from spending money past what I have in my banking account and tracks my cash transactions so I don't have to remember later why the ten-dollar bill is gone from my purse and all I have is a handful of change instead.

2. **I double up on the reminders.** Whenever I put anything in the oven, I turn on the oven light as well. Since I am in and out of the kitchen constantly, this is my personal reminder that there is something in the oven that might burn if I am otherwise occupied and don't hear the ring of the kitchen timer. And because I often go downstairs or outside to take care of another project while the oven is on, I carry a second pocket timer with me to help me remember I have put something in the oven.

3. **I always look at myself in a full-length mirror** before going anywhere. I have noticed undone skirt zippers, white threads on black skirts, and many a nylon run with this simple and extremely important routine. "Look before you leave" has become part of my dressing routine before I walk out the door every day.

While these are only small adjustments, I have learned to understand my limitations and my frailties. I can work around and above and beyond them. If you have something you regularly forget, beat your own RAM and figure out a new habit to help you remember.

For example, I run a fan every morning to freshen the air in a remote room of my house. Once I turned the fan on and completely forgot about turning it off. It ran merrily for a good twelve hours before I came back into that room again. Now when I turn on the fan, I place a bright pink handkerchief on the stairs where I will be sure to see it as my reminder: "Turn off the fan!"

Take a few minutes to identify the forgetfulness challenges that seem to accompany your stressful hours. Then keep yourself up and running by using little tricks like these to help your RAM along. Maybe someday we will be able to remember everything, but for now we will have to trick ourselves into keeping it together.

38

Plan on Replanning

broke my tooth one Tuesday morning. I was eating buttered toast, drinking milk, and enjoying a handful of raisins when all of a sudden I felt a rock in my mouth. I was feeling frustrated at the bread company for leaving rocks in their bread dough, when I felt a rough spot with my tongue and realized the rock was from my own mouth.

So, when your day starts out bad and the week looks to be even worse, what do you do? In the case of my broken tooth, I needed to make several dentist appointments, which not only fouled up my neatly planned weekly schedule, but also required changes to the next week's schedule, too.

What are we to do when the week unravels on us? Plan again. Yes, you planned the week once as though it was going to be normal. Simply plan it again with it being abnormal. I have found that replanning is always best done on paper. What will you serve for dinner if you suddenly don't have time to make anything nice? How you will get your errands done? Which errands can remain undone?

Stopping for a minute to take stock of which tasks will have to be left undone, which tasks will be done with less aplomb, and which tasks will have to be delayed altogether is essential to survival of the most organized person. Whether you break a tooth, get a flat tire, or find the store is out of stock of what you went there to buy, "adjustment" is necessary and a great skill to develop!

So, when your planned week unplans itself, call the dentist, get the best appointment they have open, and plan your week around this new reality. It doesn't do much good to complain, and you certainly can't glue your broken tooth back alone, so plan and replan you must.

Being flexible with ourselves and our schedules, and being forgiving of others' need to replan their schedules, is what makes each day such an adventure of surprises and delights. You just never know what you will find in your breakfast tomorrow.

39

The Quarterly Review
to Organize You

The seasons seem to change so quickly! When I see my first crocus beaming low from the ground, I know it is time to stop, evaluate, and plan for March, April, and May. When the fireworks stands first appear on empty lots, it is time to plan for June, July, and August. When the leaves change color, it is time to think about September, October, and November. And when turkeys are on sale, it is time to think through December, January, and February. If we don't take time each quarter to look ahead at the next three months, things can quickly get out of hand. But when we do a quarterly review, we can easily plan and prepare for what each new season will bring.

Whatever time of year it is, pull out a current calendar and take a look ahead. Get a feel for the pacing, pressures, and preparations that will be needed during the next three months. For example, spring often means there will be five major events that need our attention: Spring Vacation, Easter, Mother's Day, Memorial Day, and sometimes a graduation or two.

Here is an easy method to help you organize and prepare for these events.

Take five pieces of lined 8½" x 11" paper, fold each of them into quarters, and entitle each sheet for one holiday: "Spring Vacation," "Easter," "Mother's Day," "Memorial Day," and "Graduation." These titles will change for the different holidays during the different seasons of the year.

Label the upper left-hand section of the paper "Questions" and the upper right-hand section "Answers." Label the lower left-hand section of the paper "Things to Do" and the lower right-hand section "Things to Buy." Without much effort, questions and answers, and things to do and things to buy will fill your mind. For example: Will you be celebrating Easter? If so, how? Will you be traveling? Are you planning to fill Easter baskets for some treasured children? Do you want to invite someone to spend the weekend with you? What activities will you do the Saturday before? How will you spend Sunday?

As the questions come into your mind, write them down in the upper left-hand side of the "Easter" page. Make sure you leave ample space between each question. Then, try to answer each of these questions (the best you can at this early stage) on the corresponding lines in the upper right-hand section of the page. At the bottom of the page, make a preliminary list of "Things to Do" and "Things to Buy."

HOLIDAY OR SPECIAL OCCASION:
MOTHER'S DAY

QUESTIONS:	ANSWERS:
Who will we invite?	Mine, his, her family
What gift for Mom?	White leather purse
What game/activities?	"Whose mom is this?"
What main menu and dessert?	Roast beef & rice Asparagus Cheesecake

THINGS TO DO:	THINGS TO BUY:
Invitations x 20	Tender roast beef, makings for cheesecake
Ask Jane for dessert recipe	Shop for purse
Find pink/blue floral arrangement for table	Favors for table
Borrow cheesecake pan	Funny hats at thrift store for game

Once you have prepared an Easter sheet, do the same for the other up-coming events: Spring Vacation, Mother's Day, Memorial Day, and Graduation.

- Do you need to decide upon a graduation gift for a special person in your life? (Maybe you can call a good friend and share in the selection and cost of a gift.)
- Do you need new duffel bags for your camping trip over Memorial Day weekend? (Maybe you can add that to your errands list this week.)
- Where will you be going for your vacation? (Maybe this is a good time to discuss it with your family.)

Keep your lists close at hand so you can conveniently write down additional questions, answers, and items needing attention. If you work best in your kitchen, put the lists on the refrigerator for the next few days to evaluate your desires and make plans. If you use a daily planner, you may want to designate some lined planner sheets for your lists. If you spend most of your time at an office, take the lists with you to work. You will be surprised at how quickly and easily you can use extra, spare moments to make notations. With these simple lists as blueprints, you can begin to consolidate your plans and focus your attentions on a successful and organized season.

You may want to do this exercise of "Stop, Evaluate, and Plan" every quarter: once at the beginning of spring (March, April, May), once at the beginning of summer (June, July, August), once at the beginning of fall (September, October, November), and once at the beginning of winter (December, January, February). This method will see you through four, three-month periods without having to do a great deal of planning in January when you are exhausted from a busy December and holiday season. It will also help you through the other three seasons with greater ease.

It is possible to plan the whole year for you and your family with ease! Simply repeat the pattern throughout the year: start early with your planning, make initial lists to get your mind rolling, and then schedule the action items into your regular routine. Any season can be better, less stressful, and more fulfilling. Start now and begin the magic of being early, relaxed, and on top of things.

40

A Closet for All Seasons

The transition of seasons and the clutter it brings to our homes can often be overwhelming. Usually, Old Man Weather fools us a bit. In the fall, he sends a sharply bitter day that sends us scurrying for our winter clothes and then laughs at us with several days or weeks of warm weather. In the spring, there is often a week of overly warm weather with temperatures that are too warm for wool. Rather than let the transition of seasons be a source of stress, let's use the changing seasons as an opportunity to sort, clean, and organize our clothes and our closets.

No matter the season, you can start bringing order to your closets. Begin by gathering three large plastic containers or sturdy cardboard boxes for storing your family's out-of-season clothing. Label two containers as "Seasonal Clothes." The third container will become your "Donations" box, which you can use all year long.

Storage containers should always be labeled on both ends so they can be easily identified in the storage area, the garage, or the attic. Wherever you store your containers, though, try to keep stacking to a minimum—it seems like the one we need is always on the bottom!

Beginning with your own wardrobe, sort through your clothes. Separate them into three general piles: "spring/summer" and "fall/winter," with the third pile—the donation pile—for items that you haven't worn for at least one year, that don't fit any more, that are worn but not worn-out, or that are out of style. If you find other items in your closet that belong elsewhere in your house, set them aside to be put away at the end of the project.

Return to your closet those items that are in season and that are your preferred classics. Take the out-of-season clothing you desire to save and fold it neatly into your labeled storage containers. Put these containers away in your storage area. Take the "Donations" box and place it in your vehicle so you can drop it off at the thrift store the next time you are out running errands. (Remember to add this item to your errands list.)

Keep a longer-sleeved shirt, light jacket, or a warm sweater in your closet year round to wear during the occasional chilly spring or fall day as the seasons transition. Children and teenagers should have a light jacket or sweater available for school and play that will keep them warm during these transition days as well.

When the seasons change, you'll know it is time to find and retrieve your stored clothing containers. For instance, when fall arrives (usually when the first winter storms come to your area), retrieve and open your "Seasonal Clothes" containers. Lay out the winter clothes and sort through them.

As always, have your "Donations" box close at hand. This is the perfect time to be ruthless with those clothes that have lingered in your storage area from year to year and no longer work for you or your family. Put them aside for charity or—should they be completely and totally useless for future wear—toss them in the wastebasket.

Then gather up your summer clothes for storage. As you transfer your summer clothes from closet to box, take a moment to identify those items suitable for donation. Hang up the winter clothes in your closet or put them in your drawers and on your shelves, and you are ready to enjoy a new season with a new wardrobe.

Inevitably you will find some stray clothing items turning up during the critical transition weeks. Consider having a small "Items to Store" container convenient to the laundry room to collect those stray out-of-season clothes. You may also wish to find a permanent place in the laundry room to store your "Donations" box, using it all year round to collect those clothes that could be appropriately donated instead of returned to your family's closets.

Finally, make a note on your calendar or in your planner two weeks from the day you rotate your clothes to remind you to pack up the clothes in your "Items to Store" box and add them to your storage area so this project can be completely finished.

When the weather changes once again, the cycle is reversed. Winter clothes are sorted, folded, and stored even as summer clothing is retrieved, sorted, and hung, put in drawers, or on shelves.

It is possible to have an orderly and organized closet. So label some containers for seasonal storage, find a space to store the out-of-season clothing, and enjoy the simplicity of an organized, functional clothing closet all year round.

41

Beat the Heat

The heat of summer often brings with it many organizational challenges, not the least of which is the added chaos from having the children home more of the time.

Here are three quick and easy ideas that can help you beat the heat and make summertime more pleasant for everyone.

1. **Prepare easy meals.** There is no need to make the kitchen hotter than necessary, especially during the later afternoon and early evening. I encourage you during the hot, hot summer days to plan meals that are simple and easy to prepare. If you are planning on heating up the kitchen or making an elaborate dinner, I would suggest preparing the meal in the morning when the house tends to be cooler and you have more energy.

2. **Take a siesta.** Designate some time after lunch to enjoy some "quiet time." Encourage each child to choose a quiet, calming activity: reading, coloring pages, even taking a short nap. No friends, no interruptions, no movies, and no phone calls. The idea is to keep the house relatively quiet and provide you with a respite during the wild and crazy days of summer heat.

When the siesta is over, back come the friends, out go the kids for a splash through the sprinklers, and up comes Mom to return to her homemaking duties. Everyone is refreshed and ready to enjoy the afternoon. Try it—it really works!

3. **Run errands early.** Schedule time first thing in the morning to go grocery shopping or run your errands. The day is different then—calmer and cooler—and you will be calmer and cooler, too. You'll find that decision making is easier and the kids are more tolerant of each other in the relative cool of the morning. With your errands out of the way early, you can be back home and safe from the sun before it really gets hot.

Summer is a great time to have fun activities with your family. And by implementing these three simple ideas, your summer mood will improve, and you will get through the hot, hectic summer months more easily and smoothly and with a happier family.

42

Rescuing Ruined Holidays

I t was Memorial Day and it was raining! What a mess! The outdoor breakfast had to come inside and we had to cancel the planned games at the park *and* the mid-afternoon hike. What do you do when the weather or other unexpected events threaten to ruin your holiday?

It is a good idea to have a backup idea in place for those crazy days when your carefully laid plans are washed away by the rain.

For example, we decided to have a winter party on that particular rainy Memorial Day. We lit up the gas fireplace and drank hot chocolate with marshmallows and ate homemade donuts. We had the children bring a blanket from their beds to the living room and had a "picnic breakfast in bed."

Instead of games at the park, we had a treasure hunt in the house. While the children scattered around the house, labeling all the rooms as different parts of an ancient castle (dungeon, great hall, jail, and princess loft), I hid a small wicker basket filled with goodies and wrote clues to lead the children to the treasure.

After hot clam chowder for lunch, we drove to the nearest grocery store, where we hiked up and down the aisles, purchasing the items necessary to bake and decorate cupcakes. We came home and made the cupcakes, delivering the extras to close friends and neighbors.

After a trip around the neighborhood delivering cupcakes, we settled down to watch a patriotic family movie and enjoy some much-needed naps. And so the day ended, completely different from, but just as good as what I had planned before I woke up that morning.

Take some time now to ask some questions that will help develop a good back-up plan. If the weather turns bad, what will you do? If someone gets sick, how will you make this a great holiday anyway? If something goes wrong and your plans go awry, what might you do instead? What can you do on a rainy Memorial Day, a Halloween night with everyone sick with colds, or a warm and snowless Christmas Eve?

Keep a file of these alternate ideas and add to it throughout the year. Then, when you have to alter your plans due to weather, illness, or other challenges, you will always have a backup plan in place. Add a positive attitude (especially on important holidays) to your plan and you will be able to enjoy whatever unexpected event comes your way.

43

Tricks to Make Halloween a Treat

Halloween is a fun and exciting holiday. But it also often brings the stress of planning parties, making costumes, and handing out treats. Can Halloween really be a treat? Yes!

1. **Making costumes.** Dressing up for Halloween is one of the best parts of the holiday. So begin by making a list of everyone in your family who will need a costume. Then hold a brief family discussion to discuss what each family member wants to be for Halloween. Review what costumes you have in storage that could be worn again before you go to the effort and expense of making or buying new costumes. For those members of your family that do need new costumes, discuss how much time will be spent preparing the costumes and how much the budget will allow for each costume. Encourage your children to choose costumes that are both simple to make and that can be saved and reused by other members of your family the next year.

Look at your family calendar. It is never too early to begin working on costumes, selecting masks or makeup, and preparing the whole family for the big day. Keep the costumes as simple as possible, always designing, purchasing, or making them with the goal of storing them for use again and again.

I recommend starting with your youngest child and working up to your oldest. Not only will it probably be the easiest costume to make, it will help keep your stress level low by starting with something small. Your older children will probably want a costume with a more elaborate design, but remember that you may have to match that standard with each subsequent costume you purchase or make.

It is a good idea to choose simple, classic costumes for yourself and your spouse, ones that can be worn year to year without much fuss or hassle. For instance, I have a good friend who is a queen for Halloween every year. She has invested in a braided hair piece, a set of large faux pearls, and a flowing, multi-colored robe with a delicate golden chain that hangs from her belt. Her husband is often dressed as a wizard with a hat, false beard, and star-studded robe. Both costumes fit easily into the same container and can be slipped on with ease.

2. **Handing out treats.** There are two important decisions to make about Halloween candy: What will you give out? What will you do with all the candy that your children bring home?

There are so many choices for Halloween treats. Choose a candy that suits your family so that any leftovers can be enjoyed at the next family celebration or special event. If you don't want to give candy, try handing out something like quarters, a toothbrush, or another children's treasure.

But what about all the candy that comes home with your children? Allow your children to enjoy some of the candy on Halloween night, but then gather the remaining candy in a collective pot that can be brought out to share and enjoy on subsequent evenings or family gatherings. This method helps keep the dentist at bay and the candy all in one place during the next several months.

3. **Planning dinner.** Halloween is a busy night, so plan to prepare an easy, filling dinner. I like to serve hot soup (which I begin cooking in my Crock-Pot during the calmer, earlier hours of the day and keep hot until dinner) and bake breadstick "bones."

When Halloween is over, pack away the costumes as neatly as possible in sturdy containers. Purchased masks will last longer if they are kept in smaller, individual boxes inside the larger container. Label the containers on both ends and put them away until next October.

Make every Halloween a happy—and organized—holiday.

44

The Gift of Simplicity

Christmas may be the hardest holiday of the year. We are often too busy, despite our best efforts, to slow down and enjoy the season. We seem to spend so much of the holiday acquiring and accumulating things that fill our closets, our homes, and our lives that we really don't need and either don't want or don't use. And then we are left exhausted and strangely unhappy.

If this scenario sounds familiar, may I encourage you to reverse this trend in a small way? Here are three simple things you can do right now to reduce the acquisition and accumulation addiction that threatens to overwhelm your holiday season:

1. **Keep it simple.** Commit to go simple this year. For instance, instead of lots of gifts for lots of people, choose one or two special gifts per person for your immediate family, a group gift for those at work, and a small standard gift for those friends and neighbors who come to the door to exchange holiday greetings.

2. **Keep it practical.** As you draw up your gift list, think of items that are more tools than trinkets. Think preparation, emergencies, and maybe even service. Buy slippers for cold mornings when the heater is still rumbling to life, small LED emergency flashlights for employees, and

a box of emergency wooden matches in a resealable clear plastic jar for neighbors and nearby friends. Give your spouse or best friend a book with ten free "Put away your wash" or "Fix your favorite dinner" or "Wash the truck" service coupons.

3. **Keep it personal.** Encourage your family members to bypass the mall and give each other small, simple homemade gifts instead. Not only will it increase creativity, but it also allows for personalization and often produces the most treasured gift of all. (I still keep the homemade top my father made for me from a wooden spool when I was a child.)

So this holiday season, look for ways to stay away from the store, stay away from spending money, and stay away from falling into the acquisition and accumulation trap. Life is not about owning—it is about loving. It is not about keeping—it is about giving. Focus on *giving*, and this season will be better, you will be happier, and everything will be simpler for you and for those you love.

45

Making Christmas Memories

Do you want your holiday season to be more memorable? Do you want to look past the gift giving, decorating, and entertaining, and make the Christmas season more purposeful and meaningful for your family?

As I have thought about holidays past, it seems that the best memories I have are of *doing* something special—not receiving, not entertaining, not decorating. Choose one of these four ideas that will help you *do something* this season, and begin making some special holiday memories as a family.

1. **Take an hour and cook something together as a family.** It doesn't have to be elaborate or difficult. Just cooking a Tuesday night dinner together can be memorable. The important thing is to do it together.

Or perhaps you might use the time to teach your children how to make your favorite simple homemade candy. These treats could then be wrapped and shared with friends, neighbors, and associates.

2. **Take an hour to make a simple craft project.** You can make a simple garland by punching a hole in the corner of some old Christmas cards and stringing them on brightly-colored yarn with some ribbons and small jingle bells as accessories. It might be just the thing to give as a gift to an elderly person, a bedridden person, or even the widower down the

street. Again, it is not so important *what* you decide to do, but rather that the family is involved together. Creating something unusual and interesting is a good way for your family to have a "Christmas to remember."

3. **Take an hour and visit someone who is alone or in need.** Take flowers to someone in the hospital. Sing Christmas carols to the widow next door. Volunteer to help with dinner service at the homeless shelter. No matter where you are, give those around you some extra love, time, and attention.

4. **Take an hour to do anonymous service.** It might be driving to the local park and picking up trash, or to a church to clean the exterior walks, or leaving an anonymous envelope full of restaurant coupons in the mailbox of a family in need. Consider your service a "gift to the world at large."

If you can devote some time to one of these four "memory-making hours" (or maybe all four), in the midst of shopping, entertaining, and preparing for the holiday season, you'll find you'll have a special holiday to remember indeed. Instead of talking about the gifts they got, the family will talk of the time the powdered sugar exploded all over Mom's eyebrows while they made candy, or the fun Christmas card they used in the garland. They will remember helping at the homeless shelter, and they will never drive past that special family's mailbox again without smiling a little inside.

Make time to *do something* this Christmas season and enjoy making memories together. It will bring order to your holidays.

ORGANIZE YOUR OTHER IMPORTANT OCCASIONS

46

Road Trip!

Whether you are traveling on a daytrip or a week-long journey, a family road trip can be an enjoyable and memorable vacation—especially if you plan ahead and keep things organized. Here are four easy tips to help your vacation turn out right: Plan, Prepare, Pack, and Review.

1. **Plan.** Begin by titling a sheet of paper "Our Trip." Divide the sheet into several columns, one for "Mom & Dad" and one for each child. As items you need to pack come to mind, add them to the list in the appropriate column. You will be surprised how many ideas will occur to you. Post the sheet on your refrigerator or keep it in your planner. Then, as you go about your daily routine, continue to add items as you think of them. When the actual packing day arrives, you will have a complete and thorough list ready to use.

2. **Prepare.** A few days before you begin packing, take a few minutes to prepare the vehicle. Unload everyday needs so there will be plenty of room for this longer trip. A clean car is easier to pack and is nicer to ride in during a long road trip. Plus, you can rest assured that your regular, everyday items are safe at home and not lost along the way.

As you pack the car, remember to include some smaller plastic bags in

141

your glove compartment for the inevitable "I'm feeling sick" comment and some wet wipes to clean up should an accident truly happen. Designate a paper lunch sack or a plastic grocery bag as the "trash bag" and position one in the front, middle, and rear seating of the car. It is also a good idea to bring along an "activity bag," filled with small activities or surprises that you can use whenever the children are restless, bored, or begin to argue. If you have the space in your car, you may decide to let each child pack their own "activity bag" with their own small treasures and entertainment items.

3. **Pack.** Two words: Travel light. Most families pack about twice as much clothing than they actually need when they travel. Instead, as you prepare your packing list, pick and choose articles of clothing that will work in many situations. Picking outfits that you can mix and match will save on time and space. Remember, you are not moving, you are just traveling!

Help your children pack using the same methods. Review with them their column on the master "Our Trip" list and discuss the specific details. Limit the number of items they can take. For instance, a three-day trip might require packing one pair of shoes, three shirts, one skirt or pair of pants, three sets of underwear, three pairs of socks, and one jacket or sweater (including the items they are wearing).

Assign suitcases to each member of the family. If you don't have a suitcase for each of the children, specify two or more children to share one suitcase. Or, if you are planning on using fewer pieces of larger luggage for the entire family, have each child put each day's worth of clothing (shirt, pants, socks, underwear) in a large, clear plastic bag labeled with their name. Store these bags together in a larger suitcase. Then, when it's time to get dressed for the new day on the road, out comes the bag with today's clothing, the child can get dressed easily, the dirty clothes go back in the bag, and your luggage stays organized.

Some families even skip the suitcases altogether and use standard-sized boxes with sturdy lids instead because these boxes stack nicely in the rear of their vehicle. Each box is labeled on all four sides with the names of one or two children so retrieval is easy and convenient.

On packing day, have family members gather their toiletries, put them in another bag labeled with their name, and then put those bags (along with their pajamas and one set of clean underwear) in an "overnight" suitcase. This suitcase is the last put in the vehicle. Having these items all in one place will help if your family is staying overnight in a hotel or with a family member before reaching your final destination. With a well-packed overnight bag, only one suitcase has to be retrieved instead of unpacking the whole car.

4. **Review.** When you arrive home from your trip, take a moment to review the successes and learn from the missteps. What did you take that you didn't need? What did you have to buy along the way because you didn't pack it? What snacks worked well for this trip (and which didn't)? Keep careful notes about each trip with your "Master Trip List" so that you will be able to refer to them when you plan your next road trip. I like to put my "Master Trip List" on index cards and keep them in the back of my recipe box. They are easy to retrieve and I can use them over and over again.

Each and every time you begin to pack, pull out your "Master Trip List" and use it as the basis for the new trip's planning and packing. You will occasionally add an item here or there to meet the needs of a particular adventure, but for the most part, you will be able to rely on the permanent list to make sure and confident decisions.

47

Moving Your Home in Six Easy Steps

Congratulations! You're planning on moving to a new location! Now what? How can you prepare for this important change in your life? Where do you even begin?

Moving is a stressful situation: You usually need to be ready to be out of the residence in thirty days or so, and yet you want to maintain a semblance of "ordinary living" in the meantime. I have developed a workable plan for pre-packing and living out of boxes that may be just what you are looking for. Remember, as with any big job, start small and work in stages.

1. **Begin gathering supplies.** Your moving boxes should be easy to open and close and be stackable and sturdy. My favorite boxes are the copy paper boxes, which can be found at copy centers and are often free for the asking. I also like using produce boxes from the local grocery store.

If free boxes are not available, purchase the best you can afford. Select boxes that are similar in size, shape, and durability. This will make them easier to stack and store. Investing in sturdy boxes can be a long-term solution, as these same boxes can be used as storage boxes once you have moved. You will also need some clear packing tape to secure the boxes once they are full, and two thick black marking pens.

2. **Begin collecting items to discard or donate.** Go through your

closets and cupboards, one shelf, one drawer, and one closet rod at a time. Discard or give away as much as possible. You don't want to go to the work of packing, moving, and unpacking something just to wonder why you went to all that trouble when you could have just given it away. Now is the time to be ruthless. Give away, give away, give away!

3. **Begin packing nonessential items.** Pack away items that are not essential to your everyday living. These may include sentimental treasures, books (which should be packed in smaller boxes so they are easy to lift and transport), craft supplies, out-of-season clothing, and some of your children's toys. Remember to keep like items with like items so that unpacking will be as easy as packing.

As you pack a family member's treasures, try to keep each person's items in separate boxes, even if it means that some of the boxes remain open for a time or mixing unlike items in the same box. Then, when a family member's box is full, tape it, label it, and stack it. This will make unpacking much easier at the other end.

4. **Label the boxes.** Using a permanent marking pen and writing in large, easy-to-read letters, indicate the contents of each box. Label each box on both ends and on the top. This "triple" labeling may seem like extra work, but it is well worth the trouble in the long run because it will increase the visibility of your labels no matter how the boxes get moved around or stacked. If you need to retrieve something you have packed away before you actually move, you will have an easier time locating it in a clearly labeled box. This also helps ensure the right boxes end up in the right room for unpacking.

You may also wish to print out several copies of room labels ("Kitchen," "Master Bedroom," "Bathroom," or "Upstairs Hall Closet") and tape them to the appropriate boxes when you seal them up.

5. **Start stacking boxes.** Stack your newly packed boxes along a bedroom wall, in the garage, or in the basement. Try to keep all the boxes from a specific room or area of your house together. Stack the boxes in two rows outward from the wall, leaving slender aisles in between. This configuration will allow you to access the boxes in the back more easily

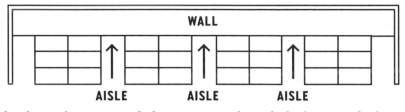

and reduces the time needed to rummage through the boxes to find something you may have already packed.

6. **Repeat as needed.** Now having done the initial packing, start the process again: sort, discard or donate, and pack. Once the first round of packing is finished, you will see many other things that really aren't essential to your everyday functioning and could easily be discarded, donated, or packed.

This method of packing will make your home look neater, bigger, and less cluttered—all real benefits when persuading a potential buyer that your house is the right one for them. And by pre-packing, you will have less daily housework prior to your move because many of your belongings are already in boxes.

Whenever the decision to move is made, begin packing *now!* There will be enough stress making arrangements, renting a truck, and finding a new place to live. Don't let packing be part of the problem. Instead, make it part of the process.

48

Wedding Presents and Gift Giving

B ecause celebrations are ever present in our lives, it is a good idea to think about organizing your gift giving practices, especially for weddings, though these same principles apply to almost all kinds of gift giving.

When I work with families trying to become more organized, we often discuss the three levels of wedding gift giving: close friends and family, good friends and family, and obligatory gifts. You can be more organized if you decide early what to give in these different situations.

1. **Close friends and family.** Wedding gifts for our close friends and family will tend to be more expensive and more elaborate. It is likely they can either be hand-delivered or that we won't mind the expense of sending them in the mail.

2. **Good friends and family.** We probably won't spend as much time or money on gifts for our good friends and family, but we still care about their quality and appearance. We will be less likely to want to expend too much energy shopping for these gifts or using funds sending gifts through the mail.

3. **Obligatory gifts.** These gifts are for acquaintances, business associates, professional friends, the children of good friends, and others with

whom we have fewer emotional ties. It is appropriate for us to give a gift, but the smallest amount of money and energy should be spent on these gifts.

As you plan your gift giving strategy, you will also need to make some financial decisions such as, How many of each kind of such gifts can you anticipate will be needed for the upcoming year? How will we include the cost of these gifts as part of our budget? Which gifts can we hand-deliver and which can we mail?

It seems that when it comes to wedding gifts, many couples can identify a certain gift they did not receive on their wedding day but which they very much wished they had received. That gift might be the best item for them to give. For instance, my husband and I did not receive a garden hose for our wedding, so it's become a tradition for us to give garden hoses as wedding gifts to close friends and family when we personally attend the wedding. We purchase a gift card to a home improvement store for good friends and family with a greeting card encouraging them to buy a garden hose. We also give a smaller gift card to those to whom we have obligations or when we need to send wedding congratulations through the mail.

Because we have standardized our wedding gift giving, we often purchase several garden hoses when they are on sale, saving us time and money. We also purchase some gift cards from the home improvement store in two different amounts and keep them with a stack of wedding congratulations cards.

We attach a large bow and a greeting card to the garden hose and keep the wedding invitation with the hose to remind us where and how to get to the wedding and reception. The gift cards are put inside greeting cards and tucked inside the envelopes. The gift card amount is written in pencil in the upper right-hand corner of the envelope to remind us of what is inside.

Take a few moments and think about what you would like to give as a gift on a regular basis. How could you tailor this desire to fit the three different categories of wedding gifts? When is the next sale on that gift coming up?

This is a simple and easy way to help your gift giving budget and it will definitely make your life easier all year long!

49

Preparing for the Unexpected

Unexpected surprises come all the time, sometimes during the summer months and often during the winter holiday season. They usually fall into three categories: unexpected overnight guests who need accommodating; an unexpected meal that needs to be just a little nicer than your usual fare; and unexpected entertainment needs. Plan for the unexpected now and you can relax, knowing you are prepared for anything.

1. **Unexpected guests.** Designate a drawer or box to store supplies for when company comes. This might include a set of clean sheets and pillowcases, fluffy towels, a fresh tube of toothpaste with several unopened spare toothbrushes, a bottle of fancy lotion, and a wrapped bar of sweet-smelling soap. You may also include some small paper cups and a pretty box of tissues. Then, when company comes unexpectedly, welcome them heartily and while they are visiting with the rest of the family, you can quickly and easily prepare for their stay. Just pull out your "company" drawer or box and you'll find all your supplies ready and waiting. Your company will feel special and appreciated because of your thoughtfulness, and you can enjoy their surprise visit instead of having to run to the store to gather supplies!

2. **Unexpected meals.** It is always helpful to plan ahead for a "company" meal. The meal should be a menu that can be assembled from supplies you have on hand at all times and be easy to prepare. For myself, I usually serve canned ravioli, along with frozen, buttered green beans, garlic toast, and a homemade raisin cookie cake that only takes thirty minutes to prepare, bake, and serve.

Knowing exactly what you will serve when company shows up unexpectedly means you won't be in a panic, have to make a quick trip to the store, or feel pressured to eat out (which is fine on occasion but can be hard on the budget if you haven't planned for it). It also means you will be able to relax when the doorbell rings. "Come in," you can say with a smile. "Won't you please stay for dinner?"

3. **Unexpected entertainment needs.** Often when unexpected company comes it's fun to have a short activity ready that can involve them in easy conversation, maybe keep their children focused, or sometimes even make them more comfortable with your own family members. It might be wise to have both an indoor and an outdoor activity in mind with supplies at hand.

For instance, a good friend of mine keeps a special stick and string with a bottle of dishwashing soap readily available to blow large and fancy bubbles in the back yard as a fun and memorable activity. She also knows a simple and fun drama game that can accommodate groups of all sizes. Her early preparation and organization makes her company comfortable in her home no matter the season or the occasion.

When you are prepared for the unexpected, you can host your special guests, serve an elegant meal in thirty minutes, or even provide a fun activity when it is needed. So relax and enjoy the occasion that brings visitors to your door!

50

Serving at a Time of Sorrow

When my sweet cousin died, I discovered I wasn't as organized and prepared to help as I would have wished. I hadn't prepared myself sufficiently to serve at a moment's notice others who were also suffering from the loss.

It is hard to know how to prepare for such an event, but I would like to suggest three ways we can organize ourselves better so as to always be ready to serve. Service will almost always be needed when you already have a packed schedule, other commitments, or some heavy emotional demands of your own. If you have made some simple preparations, it will be easier to respond to the need and to show your love to the bereaved.

1. **Give a simple gift.** Simple silk flower arrangements, scented candles, or other small, appropriate gifts are a beautiful way to tell someone you care. You can purchase these items in bulk and keep them wrapped, ready to take with you to the home of the bereaved when you visit. These gifts don't need to be fancy or large or expensive, but they can remind the family (sometimes for a long time to come) of a dear friend who offered comfort and love.

Please know that just because you don't know what you will say, or even if you don't know that you will be able to say anything for your own tears, it is important to *just go!* Having been on the other side of grief, I know that the people who are bereaved need to tell their story again, need to cry again, and need to share their feelings again. You can help in that process by going and listening.

2. **Give a tasty treat.** Have a simple, edible treat prepared, stored, and ready to share with the family or guests who might be coming to stay. This treat would ideally be something that could stay out on the counter without failing, spoiling, or needing much attention. A good neighbor of mine always keeps some prepared cinnamon rolls in her freezer, ready to bake and take at a moment's notice. Oh, how good they tasted to those who were hungry but had no energy to prepare food!

3. **Give an uplifting card.** Keep a selection of condolence cards handy. You can add a personal note and quickly send your greetings and feelings to the bereaved by mail. Those who mourn are waiting for your concern, your love, and your written messages. It buoys them up through the long days after the death and funeral.

When our son died, I waited for one of my close relatives to write. I don't why it was important to me to know she cared, but when I received her personal note penned inside the card, I was better able to cope, knowing her strong arms of caring were around me.

Of course, you may want to do something more personal the next time death comes close, but being ready with small gifts of caring to give at a moment's notice will make it more peaceful for you when life's other obligations are also knocking and there is just no time to stop, think, or shop.

51

When Change Comes Charging Through

There was a period of my life when some major changes came charging through. I won't go into details, but I spent long days sorrowing, trying to comprehend these overwhelming changes. After having gone through that experience, I learned some lessons about keeping order in my life while adjusting to a major shift in my reality. May I share what I learned?

1. **Go slowly.** When change is suddenly thrust upon you, it is important—even essential—to *go slowly*. Yes, keep to the routines you trust and know as a part of your life. Eat the same foods you have always enjoyed, wear clothes that fit loosely and are comfortable, and, most important, don't make any major decisions about your current situation. The changes which have been thrust upon you are enough for now.

2. **Let others help.** Those close to you want to help you through this difficult time. Let them help you with the dishes, with the wash, and with the housecleaning. You may still need to supervise, to be involved, and to coordinate, but let others take over the work. You hadn't expected this change that suddenly, quite unexpectedly, has made everything different in your entire life. You need to cry, take long walks, and heal.

3. **Keep a list.** There will be things that come to your mind that will

need your attention—maybe even items that are critical to keep life running smoothly—and there are others that can wait until you are through the worst of it and can resume your life at a more normal pace. Add everything you think of to that list so that when you do surface again, you can return to your days with some guidance. During my time of major change, I kept my "To Do Someday" list in the front of my planner. Then, when someone called and asked if they could help in any way, I replied in the positive and searched down my list until I found something appropriate for the situation. "Would you mind picking up my dry cleaning for me?" "How about weeding my front boardwalk?" "Would it be possible for you to substitute for me on Tuesday?" When friends and acquaintances ask to help, let them. Even the smallest bits of help go a long way to alleviate your stress and fill you with support and love.

4. **Listen to your body.** When it needs to eat, eat. When it needs to sleep, slip away into a quiet room and let it rest. When you need to mourn, cry and cry and cry. The days will get brighter, shorter, and easier to walk through, but when sudden change demands you walk through the gauntlet of emotion, respond as your body demands.

Someday soon you will be able to function at your highest level again. But when change charges into your life, go slowly, mourn as needed, let others help, and listen to your body. May brighter, more ordered days be around the corner for all of us.

52

Did I Tell You I Love You?

had a good friend who had cancer, survived and thrived after a bone marrow transplant, but eventually relapsed. I watched her hair come and go during her many treatments. I admired her courage to face the challenge of living when her will to live was sapped by fatigue and discouragement. She had the same kind of cancer our youngest son had, so I knew some of what she was going through.

When we saw one another, she usually greeted me with a "Hello, friend!" She couldn't always remember why or where she knew me, but I loved her and I wanted her to know of my feelings sooner rather than later, especially before it was too late!

Do you have some unfinished "love you" business in your life? If so, do yourself a favor. The next time you are at the store, buy a package of small note cards (your message doesn't need to be long to be meaningful). Come home and put stamps and a return address on each of the envelopes. Put each note card inside the flap of each envelope and put these "love note packets" in a convenient place ready to serve you.

Now you have a beautiful card at hand for those moments when you want to tell someone you love how much they mean to you. It's easy and quick to write a short note, seal and address the pre-stamped envelope.

There may be times when an e-mail or phone call can accomplish the same purpose, but for many people there is something nicer about holding a tangible envelope, seeing your handwriting, and reading a cheery note.

Keeping up with your "love yous" keeps your mind at peace. I try to always keep a supply of cheery note cards, envelopes, and stamps on my list so I can send out my messages of love without delay. You can, too!

Conclusion

L ife is hard. You can leave it that way or you can make it easier!" A friend once said this to my husband. He has had his share of life's challenges and experiences, some of them not too pleasant, but most of them now resolved and easier. From his point of view, it was this statement urging him to take what life handed him and make it nicer, happier, and better that has made all the difference.

So I pose this last question: In the end, would you rather take your hard life (and all your places of disorder, disarray, and chaos) and leave it that way, or would you like to make your life easier?

Knowing how your heart will respond, may I encourage, implore, and otherwise influence you to take the first step: open the first messy drawer, face the big junky closet, or walk into that cluttered laundry room and begin to make your life easier and more organized?

I know you can change from where you are now to where you want to be. No, I don't promise your laundry will always be caught up, or your spouse will always remember to take out the trash, or your teenagers will begin to clean up their rooms without being asked. But I will promise that for you and for me, there can be an easier, more orderly life. It is up to us, so let's make it happen!

About the Author

Marie Ricks has been sharing home organization skills since 1986 when she began teaching an eight-week, sixteen-topic course including time management, food preparation, closet and cupboard organization, budgeting, teaching children to work, and shopping skills.

Her classes have proven popular, and she frequently teaches home organization principles to individuals and groups of all sizes, including at Brigham Young University and BYU–Idaho Education Week.

Marie has published a *House of Order Handbook,* which has printed "organization" materials to help home managers, whatever their needs may be. (See www.houseoforder.com for more information about all of Marie's organizational products.)

Marie writes a column for the *Deseret Morning News* and has had her own radio show on AM820. She currently appears as a featured guest on *Studio 5,* a weekday talk show on KSL-TV. She shares a weekly "House of Order" newsletter for interested women from her Web page (www.houseoforder.com), and records a weekly podcast segment for Mormon MomCast.com.

She loves to scrap quilt, make pressed-flower greeting cards for friends and family, and write personal histories. She has more than 300 home management books in her personal library.

She has been happily married to Jim Ricks for 35 years and together they are the parents of five sons. Marie and her family live in Highland, Utah, where she and her husband garden in the summer and share wood-working projects in the winter.